THOUGHTS HELD HOSTAGE

DEBRA WATKINS

THOUGHTS HELD HOSTAGE

*A Black Teacher's Journey
of Unlocking Young Minds*

DEBRA WATKINS

ABEN BOOKS

CALIFORNIA

ABEN BOOKS

A Black Education Network (ABEN)
P.O. Box 3134
San Jose, CA 95156
(408)977-4188 or info@caaae.org

For information about special discounts for bulk purchases, please contact CAAAE at (408)977-4188 or info@caaae.org.

Debra Watkins is available for live events and speaking engagements. For more information, or to book your event, contact (ABEN), P.O. Box 3134, San Jose, CA 95156, or at (408)977-4188, or email at: info@caaae.org.

Interior Design by Wanda Lee-Stevens, wandaleestevens.com
Jacket by Malcolm McCrae, Artist, Author, Educator, Speaker

Manufactured in the United States of America

10 9 8 7 6 5 4 3 2 1

Library of Congress Cataloging-in-Publication Data is available.

ISBN 978-0-9976821-6-8 (Paperback Edition) Second Edition
ISBN 978-0-9976821-5-1 (E-book)

DEDICATION

This book is dedicated to my brother, Pleaz Henry Matthews, Jr., whose genius was never fully realized, and to my extraordinary mother, Rosie Mae Masters, whose great love still resides in the hearts of her children, grandchildren and great-grandchildren.

ACKNOWLEDGEMENTS

Because my healthy village is large, I am bound to miss someone in this space. Please forgive me ahead of time if your name does not show up here, but you know who you are and the role that you played in helping me bring this book to life.

From the onset, I want to thank God for guiding the footsteps of my life. Even when valleys were low and I strayed from His side, God's steadfast faith in me never wavered.

I was blessed with a large family. It might not have seemed like a blessing when we were growing up and had to share bunk beds sometimes, but I am grateful for my sisters (Frances Wilson, Lilly Daniel, Sharon James, Candace Matthews, Janie Chavers, and Cicely Galbreath—we call her Peaches and Cathy!) and mom's tenth and final child (Keith Chavers) for allowing me to tell part of "our" story from my perspective. If I did not get some facts right, please credit my head and not my heart.

I want to thank my beautiful, only child (Alicia Watkins Okoh) for sharing me with thousands of other children while she was growing up and I was fulfilling God's purpose for my life and for gifting me with a precious granddaughter who is the light of my life and my heartbeat, Imade (pronounced E-Mah-Day). I am grateful for my son-in-law (Patrick Okoh) who married his childhood sweetheart and blessed me with his parents (Willie and Anthonia Okoh) and siblings (Imade, Ify and Edeki Okoh). I love showing his parents around California on their summer visits from Nigeria.

There are teachers who were amazing colleagues on my journey: Sue Fialer (one of my very best friends), Sharon Morales, Linda Flournoy, Dorothy Hines, and Deborah Raymond. They helped me have a story to tell.

Chris Norwood was the biggest cheerleader for this book. He planted the idea of me writing about my journey when we worked with the first cohort of Project WORD students at Oak Grove High School. The second biggest cheerleader was April Gill. After I first announced that the book was "finished" when it actually was not, April would gently prod me with a sweet text inquiry about whether or not it had been published. I would tell her just to keep me in her prayers. She did!

Dr. Gail Lasker Whaley allowed me to use her beautiful vacation home in Oxnard for 10 days in 2014 where I actually wrote the first few chapters. Gail was the first person to read Chapter 1 and gave great feedback.

Chike Akua was a solid adviser. I went to him for all kinds of advice on how to get a book published and he was never impatient with me. He answered all of my questions and provided concrete guidance. He even introduced me to the illustrator of my book's cover—the immensely talented Malcolm McCrae.

There are scholarly types who are always pushing me toward excellence. Words fail to express how deep my gratitude is for their faith in my abilities to do great work: Dr. Joyce King, Dr. John Browne. Dr. Arnetha Ball, Dr. Iva Carruthers, and Dr. Stephen Hancock. If Dr. King had her way, I would have finished a doctorate years ago. A word about Dr. Hancock. He is my "book" role model. He has already outlined the second book focused on the Dr. Frank S. Greene Scholars Program (GSP). I am looking forward to editing it with him and allowing some of the GSP's amazing parents to write the chapters about their experiences in our award-winning STEM program.

Carlene Pratt has been a very close friend for more than 40 years. Her sons (Edward, III and

Christopher) are my godsons. Even though she has been battling multiple myeloma for nearly 20 years, her rock solid faith in God has enabled her to pray me through all kinds of experiences. I am sure this book is one of them. Carlene and Ed have been married nearly 30 years.

Words are inadequate to fully convey my deepest gratitude for the amazing Wanda Lee-Stevens. I first met her several decades ago through her husband, Chester, whose community activism I greatly admired. I re-connected with Wanda in 2015 when mutual friends (Ron and Brenda Arthur) invited me to their home to hear Wanda read excerpts from her first book and do a book signing. As they say, the rest is history. Wanda has been an incredibly patient editor and publisher.

Lastly, I want to thank the thousands of children whose lives I have been blessed to touch through the classroom or in programs that I started outside of the classroom. Without them, most of this book would not have been possible.

Table of Contents

INTRODUCTION

When I graduated from Stanford's Teacher Education Program in June 1977, I was convinced that I was going to successfully reach every student who entered my classroom doors. I was in for a rude awakening. Not every student was eager to drink from my font of knowledge.

About eight years into my career, I was given the opportunity to teach in a brand new program called the Electronics Academy. Located on the same Independence High School campus in San Jose, California, where I had started teaching in 1977, I loved the idea of being the sole English teacher for a cohort of students for their entire high school career. My colleagues thought I was crazy! "What if you don't like some of the students?" they asked. **I said that if you don't like students you should not be teaching in the first place!** They also said that it placed a heavy burden on me if my students did not know how to write and read well by the time they graduated. I embraced the challenge.

1

Thus began my love affair with the cohort model. It would be replicated in Project WORD (Working On Redefining our Destiny), and the Dr. George Washington Carver and Dr. Frank S. Greene Scholars programs that you will read more about in the chapters that follow.

As I have traveled around the United States talking about my work, I have been asked over and over to write a book about it. Because I had such a wonderful experience with students in the Electronics Academy and in Project WORD, I finally decided to write that book. In fact, the title for this book was given to me by one of my students, Jenell Jordan, who was in the first actual cohort of Project WORD students at Oak Grove High School in San Jose. One day during a class discussion, Jenell said that people in education rarely ask students why they are not engaged with school. She said, "It is as though our thoughts are held hostage." I had promised that Project WORD cohort that I would write a book about our journey together and that I would use Jenell's title. As I started to write about the experiences, it dawned on me that I needed to start well before my teaching career ever commenced. I needed to tell my audience who helped shape my passion for all students and a special love for ones who look like me. Therefore, I begin my book with my mother. In that chapter, I try to give a glimpse into what an extraordinary woman she was in spite of a precarious start in life with a teen mother, failed marriages and the death of my oldest sister and the brother who was just 11 months younger than me. Ironically, those two were only 24 years young when their lives were tragically cut short.

I then started reflecting on those teachers who defined my school years from elementary to high school and whose lives I channeled in my own work. That is how Chapter 2 was born. It is more of a tribute to them, but beginning teachers will also learn what made them great. Hopefully, those starting their careers will benefit from these master teachers. My friends since middle school (like Jacques Bordeaux, Malcolm Green, Gary Olson, Dennise Hall) will also, no doubt, remember Mr. Kelly and Mrs. Alberts and those from my high school years (like Kathy Stolz Gorman, Jamie Perry Carter, Sue Krolak Page, Karen Oliver Olson, James Bell, Wanda Branch Kurtcu, Rocky Mayer, Silvia Quiroz) will remember Mrs. Schneider and Mr. Wooten among others.

The book was turning into a semi-memoir so I let it grow naturally. In Chapter 3, I reflected on the privilege I was afforded. From having Mr. Lahar and Mrs. Brink as high school American Field Service advisers enthusiastically recommending me for a year of study abroad in France to gaining admission to my first-choice college (Pitzer of the Claremont Colleges in California) to complete my undergraduate education to my being admitted to my first choice graduate school (Stanford

University). From this vantage point in my life, I can say with certainty that my road was, indeed, golden.

Chapter 4 covers the one career in education that I had for 35 years in the same high school district before retiring seven years early to run the California Alliance of African American Educators (CAAAE) full-time. You will read that even though I had the same career, I always sought new and challenging opportunities to engage students.

I begin Chapter 5 with a story about my brother who was murdered at age 24. While the chapter is entitled "A Few Bumps Along the Way," my brother's death was much more than an unfortunate distraction. I was so devastated by his death that I could not even talk about it for 10 years. As a veteran educator, I realize that my brother (like so many Black boys) never stood a chance at success. The school system was awfully aligned against him. When I recently shared my brother's school trajectory with a funder, he was deeply touched and suggested that I share it with others in the Fix School Discipline coalition that I have been a part of since 2013. One of these days I might. Even though my brother died in 1978, I still get very emotional when I start talking about his life. People have asked if that is why I am so passionate about serving Black children. I had never considered it, but that could play a role. Like I tell people all the time, I did this work for free for 33 years after my "day job" that paid the bills. I guess passion does look like that.

Finally, Chapter 6 is what this book was supposed to be all about when I first made that commitment to Jenell's cohort. Project WORD was such a powerful experience for me and the four men (Wilbur Jackson, Bill Nettles, Harold Clay and Bill Boone), that Wilbur and Bill actually asked if they could write this chapter. Most of what they wrote is there. I only edited a few parts. I actually enjoyed reading their perspectives on the journey. I hope that you find it instructional.

One of the most frequent comments I get is about my enormous capacity to do a lot of work at the same time! In Chapter 6, I discuss how I built several "institutions" that are still thriving. The one that I am most proud of is the Dr. Frank S. Greene Scholars Program (GSP). Thanks to incredibly committed parents, the GSP has exceeded my wildest dreams. In fact, the parent leadership is so outstanding that I am spinning off the GSP so that it becomes its own 501(c)3. As I write, the process is underway and we hope to obtain that nonprofit status by July 2016. I will have a permanent seat on the board with full voting rights so that I can help ensure that my vision for this award-winning STEM program is never compromised. When I am no longer able or interested in being engaged as a board member, the seat will pass on to my progeny to help ensure its longevity for many generations to come. How thrilling!

Never one to sit on my laurels, Chapter 8 discusses the next chapter of my work. Thanks to Dr. Joyce King's gentle prodding I have been incubating a national organization called A Black Education Network (ABEN) since 2012. With a wonderful board and brilliant scholars in our Wisdom Circle, ABEN is poised to make a huge difference for Black children throughout this country. I have come to the painful conclusion that our children live in "cultural deserts" and are dying of a thirst for the knowledge of their African past and their genius often left untapped in schools that were never designed for their success as Carter G. Woodson pointed out so many decades ago. Our vision is for ABEN to help fill that void. I am excited that the brilliant Tony Browder is one of my closest partners in this part of our work. He created the Cultural Immersion Imperative just for the students in San Jose who he started working with at Mt. Pleasant, Independence and Santa Teresa high schools during the 2015-2016 academic year. His riveting presentations have already started to have a positive effect on students who he meets with monthly. We plan to implement this model and enhance it around the country through ABEN.

After writing Chapter 8, I decided that I needed to tie up the book with a list because educators like lists and I did have a few lessons to share. I think that students studying to be teachers can benefit most from this final chapter. If they just learn from my trials and tribulations, they will be amazing educators and the world will be a better place!

Seriously, I thank God for my journey—warts and all. I am blessed to have lived long enough to see the fruits of my labor in students who have gone on to be gainfully employed as auto mechanics, personal bankers, teachers, social workers, doctors, lawyers, business men and women, and the list goes on and on. Thanks to social media, I am Friends with many of them on Facebook and some have grown children and are (hard to even write this!) doting grandparents!

While I loved ALL of my students, those in the Electronics Academy and that first cohort in Project WORD will always have extra-special places in my heart. I want to memorialize them by sharing their names below:

Abinash Kaur, Alicia Rios, Allen Brothers, Ana Mendoza, Ana Naranjo, Noah Ford, Andrew Meckler, Antoinette Cacallori, Antonio Garcia, Barry Brill, Bradley Falk, Bruno Czech, Carlos Carillo, Carlos Fuentes, Charles Dampler, Charles Webster, Chris McCann, Christian Aguilar, Christopher Young, Clark Sheuh, Connie Helms, Connie Martin, Danny Demello, Dante Houston, David Fabris, David Kabasinskas, Dawn Madrid, Desdemona Guerrero, Dorian Restrepo, Eduard Caspillo, Elvia Farias, Esther Flores, Gabriel Matsunaga, Heidi Joseph, Janet Buchan, Janet Morazan, Jeani Balagum, Jennifer Greenberg, Joe Navarro, Jose Martinez, Jose Rodriguez, Juan Nestares,

Karen Bohbot, Kenny Messenger, Kerri Macintosh, Kristine Shauer, Kuljit Sandher, Lance Hill, Lenore Carter, Leslie Griffin, Lisa Jackman, Lloyd Molina, Lorena Fewell, Luis, Villagomez, Malcolm Durham, Marcie Guitierrez, Maria Perez, Maria Rivera, Matt Lauterbach, Michael Freeman, Michael May, Nicole Shaffer, Orlino Ordono, Paula Bates, Paula Martino, Raymond Soto, Regina Sabala, Robby Stanley, Robert Sanchez, Roberta Flinn, Roger Ballelos, Santos Maraspini, Scott Suva, Shannon Gonzales, Shannon Nash, Steve Moneski, Terri Quan, Thaddeus Hammonds, Tony Gonzales, Tyronne Wells, Veronica Arzate, Victor Trujillo, Yangsook Shin, Ilhan Ahmed, Shantelle Blackburn, Jimmy Bradford, Nettie Brown, Brandon Butcher, Jenee Dampier, Kelvin (T.K.) Davis, Dejonay Etter, Matthew Grant, Tiyana Green, Rahkyta Hayes, Breanna Hunsucker, Dimitrius Jackson, Caleb Johnson, Jenell Jordan, Jolana Jordan, Scott Lawyer, Semaj Mayo, Uchenna Onyewuenyi, De'Shaun Richard, Tyrone Robinson, Sabrina Robleh, Najma Sadiq, Amadu Smart, Juquelle Thompson, Candice Wilkins, and Andre Williams.

My motto is "to whom much is given, much is required." I have been given so much in life and am honored to give back many times over. I hope you enjoy the book and are inspired to help others on your own journey.

Onward ever, backwards never!

Chapter 1

Mama

She defied the odds. Born of a 17-year old single mother in the rural South whose father, according to family lore, was killed in a hunting accident when she was just eight months old, my mother never should have amounted to much. Yet, she was extraordinary in every sense of the word. No, she did not march in the civil rights movement nor become a "first" Black in some trailblazing way. What she did was to give birth to, raise and unconditionally love ten children while weathering two challenging marriages that would have left most women despondent and defeated.

I could not write a book about my journey without first telling you about Mama. Born Rosie Mae Masters in Crockett, Texas, on November 7, 1926, my mother was the second child of that 17 year-old. My mother's brother, Marion, had been born just one year before. Yes, my grandmother, Sallie Mae Barrett, was a little wild so my mother and her brother were raised primarily by their maternal grandmother, Mollie. That, actually, was a good thing. My great-grandmother, Mollie, was one of the best cooks in Crockett and by the time my mother was seven years old, she baked her first lemon meringue pie. That talent for cooking would become a hallmark of my mother's entire life and her children and many relatives and friends were blessed by it.

One of the most influential men in my mother's entire life entered it when she was just four years old. They called him Mr. Abbey. He owned the only store in Crockett. When my grandmother got pregnant with her third child, everyone knew that Mr. Abbey was the father. One problem was that Mr. Abbey already had a wife and children. The bigger problem was that Mr. Abbey was White! When my grandmother gave birth to Aunt Bertha, Mr. Abbey was one proud father. He doted on Aunt Bertha and treated my mother and Uncle Marion like his own children. It was Mr. Abbey who told my mother to never feel inferior to White people. My mother took that to heart and passed on that same fierce pride in being Black to her own children. While Aunt Bertha was what they called "high-yella" back then and had long, naturally curly hair, my mother and her brother were dark-skinned. In that age of Jim Crowism and overt racism, it would have been easy for my mother to grow up with an inferiority complex. Even Black children called her "darky" and "nappy-haired." Yet, Mr. Abbey treated my mother and her sister like princesses and my mother grew up with a healthy self-esteem.

As an adult, my mother's best friend was actually a White woman and, quiet as kept, she often felt more comfortable around them than she did her own. This predilection informed decisions my mother would make later in her life that actually influenced where she raised her children. More about that later.

When my mother was 12 years old, she was sent to live with one of my grandmother's sisters, Mae, who lived in Los Angeles. Although Aunt Mae worked as a maid for rich White people, she managed to save enough money to buy some apartments and live quite comfortably well into old age. On a train ride back to Los Angeles from Texas during the summer before her senior year in high school, my mother met a handsome man named Pleaz Henry Matthews and soon fell in love. After graduating from Jefferson High School at 18, she married my father who was 15 years her senior. Seven children soon followed with two years between the first three and one between the last four: Linda, Frances, Lilly, Sharon, Candace, Debra and Pleaz, Jr. Although my father loved his children, he became an alcoholic and was so abusive to my mother that she left him soon after giving birth to the son he longed for after six daughters. In hindsight, I can only imagine what daily indignities and micro-aggressions my father must have suffered in a society built on the denigration of Black people and especially Black men.

The famous French author, Albert Camus, said that religion is the opiate of the people. Church figured prominently in the lives of Black people during the reign of terror called Jim Crow in this country and was, indeed, a place of refuge. My father's opiate of choice was a bottle of Ripple.

I don't recall this, but I was told that we lived in the projects until I was about three years old. The first home I remember was on Caswell Street in Compton. About the time of our move there, my mother married my stepfather, Cecil Chavers, and they had three children born three years apart: Janie, Cicily and Keith. When I was six years old, we started a pattern of moving from neighborhood to neighborhood that would last throughout my growing up years. From Compton, we lived in Monrovia, then Duarte. When I was seven, we moved to Pomona where I would live until I graduated from Pitzer College in 1976.

One of the most remarkable aspects of growing up Black in the 1960's is that my mother was intent on ensuring that her brood had experiences that most of our peers never had. While I realize now that my parents were able to rent homes in newly-integrated neighborhoods because of "White flight," we enjoyed having a backyard with a swing set and a playhouse that my skilled stepfather built from scratch. Each Christmas, he would decorate the front yard with an elaborate manger scene replete with Jesus, Mary, Joseph, angels, animals, and real hay. Bright lights illuminated that scene and colored ones set our house aglow. People came from miles around to drive slowly past the scene with such reverence that one would have thought that those people made of wood were real and worthy of praise.

Each summer we took a trip to one of California's beautiful state parks—Yosemite, Sequoia or King's Canyon. Because we were such a large family, we never really paid attention to the fact that no other Black families were at the nightly campfires where we roasted marshmallows and sang songs. Outfitted with a Coleman stove, lantern, tents, sleeping bags and ice chest, we never felt out of place in those parks and still fondly remember those summers. Twice, we took a major trip by station wagon from California to New York and back. We camped all along the way until we got to New York. In New York City, I recall us getting two hotel rooms at the end of a long hallway. I guess they were concerned that such a large group of "Negroes" might disturb the other guests! Our parents did not play so we were as quiet as church mice that night. We stayed in New York long enough to tour the Empire State building, the Statue of Liberty and Niagara Falls. In retrospect, I wonder how we managed to pass through parts of the South unscathed. Have I suppressed any negative memories?

My extraordinary mother also ensured that birthdays were celebrated and elaborate meals were had at Easter, Christmas and New Year's. Everything she made was from scratch. Famous for her fried chicken and cakes, my mother also cooked the best candied yams, macaroni and cheese, zucchini casserole, cornbread stuffing, biscuits, and yeast rolls of anyone I have ever known. If that sounds biased, you only need to ask the countless guests who were fortunate enough to partake of her fare. She knew what kind of cake each one of her children liked most and loved to make it just for them. My favorite was German chocolate, but her pound cake came in a close second. Cooking was her way of passing along love. We were showered with it.

Two tragic events shook my mother to her core and for the first time ever I thought she would lose it. Her first-born, Linda Faye, died suddenly at age 24 from a blood clot in her lungs. Linda's husband sued the doctor who had prescribed high blood pressure, diet and birth control pills and he won, but it brought little solace to Linda's four children under ten years old who were left motherless and to her devastated parents and siblings. At the time, my mother had converted to Buddhism and I can still hear the chanting ("nam myoho renge kyo") when we got the news that oppressive night as though it was yesterday. That religion saved my mother. Although she abandoned it a few years later, I am grateful that she had something to hold on to then because the next tragedy was the brutal murder of my brother. Ironically, he was also 24 at the time of his death. I recall going with my mother to tell my father that his son was dead. It was the most gut-wrenching experience I have ever had. I watched two long-divorced people holding each other and weeping over their baby. [Since my brother had been born three months prematurely, he and I were the same age for 24 days. I hated that growing up because people used to say that we were twins and I did not want to be a boy's twin. Actually, we grew to be super close and his death so crushed me that I could not even discuss it for a decade. It wasn't until I was working on my second master's degree in counseling and was asked to write a twilight journal saying goodbye to someone who I never got to say that to was I able to finally talk about my brother's murder. It would take another 25 years before I ever wrote publicly about it and that was prompted by Trayvon Martin's death. Because my brother was just another Black man, no massive hunt was launched to find his murderer. Rather than lament this for the rest of my life, I turned my anger into action and decided that his life would not be in vain. I re-committed to working on behalf of other Black boys and girls whose trajectories I could positively impact. I will discuss the lessons learned from my brother's short life in another chapter.

Although my remarkable mother gave birth to ten children, she always managed to hold a job as well. I recall when she worked as a cook at the Claremont Colleges and how proud she was years later when I graduated from one of them—Pitzer. Mostly, I remember her gradual ascent from cook to supervising cook to correctional officer (CO) over a 24-year period at the California Institution for Women (CIW)—a minimum security prison in Corona. Armed with a strong work ethic, my mother earned the respect of the inmates and her colleagues at CIW and was encouraged to become a CO. My mom studied long and hard for the CO exam and passed it with flying colors. Because my mother worked many hours and often came home dog-tired when she was a CIW cook, I took a special interest in washing her uniforms and underwear by hand, ironing the uniforms, and polishing her white shoes so that she never had to worry about that. She always expressed her gratitude. It was the very least I could do.

My mother retired from CIW at age 60 and moved to Clear Lake, California, because she loved to fish. Situated high above the Napa Valley and hours away from other family members, my mother's home became a favored destination for her children and grandchildren who braved winding roads and narrow passageways to get there. When her health began to decline 15 full and happy years after the move to Clear Lake, we "forced" her to move closer to my baby brother (Keith) and sister (Cicily) whose families lived in the Perris/Moreno Valley area. Although she fussed about the move all the time, she relished her time with them and her other children and their families who now flocked to her home there. When she declared in 2007 that this would be her last year to cook a Thanksgiving dinner, we told her that she would outlive all of us. When she passed away from a massive heart attack on New Year's Eve of that year, her children and their families were beyond devastated. Yet, we realized that she had lived a full life and was weary. We praised God for gifting us an extraordinary mother and made sure that she was wearing one of her favorite outfits at the funeral. She loved to dress and would have been pleased. What you now know about my mother is foundational for the rest of my journey. **Come along. I hope you find the ride worthwhile.**

THOUGHTS HELD HOSTAGE

Chapter 2

They Were the Ones: Teachers Who Influenced My Journey

"I've come to a frightening conclusion that I am the decisive element in the classroom. It's my personal approach that creates the climate. It's my daily mood that makes the weather. As a teacher, I possess a tremendous power to make a child's life miserable or joyous. I can be a tool of torture or an instrument of inspiration. I can humiliate or heal. In all situations, it is my response that decides whether a crisis will be escalated or de-escalated and a child humanized or dehumanized." By Haim Ginott

Elementary school was a blur except for one life-changing teacher and one profoundly dark day. Roly-poly, red-haired Mr. Stevenson was my fourth grade teacher. Since all of my teachers up to that point (and throughout my K-12 schooling) were White, I never gave it a second thought and don't recall him making a big deal of it either. He said that I was the best writer in his class so I

19

should become an English teacher. It was that simple. As the sixth of ten children, none of my siblings was old enough at the time to have attended college so I had no idea what becoming an English teacher would entail. Yet, Mr. Stevenson read my papers to the class as great examples and posted them on the bulletin board so that year I decided to fulfill his goal for me and I never wavered. Because I know firsthand what the power of a teacher's influence can be, I sought to speak bright futures into the lives of students I taught. Even those who had been discarded by traditionalists and labeled "disadvantaged", "at-risk" or "underachieving" felt valued and understood when I encouraged them to realize their genius.

Many years after fourth grade and with that image of a teacher firmly planted in my head, I stumbled upon the quote by Haim Ginott. It was such a powerful quote that I decided to distribute it to the entire staff at Oak Grove High School the year (2008) that I started coordinating Project WORD (Working On Re-defining our Destiny) on the campus. I am getting way ahead of myself and will spend much of this book writing about that specific journey, but I did not want to miss the opportunity to share that. In short, teachers sometimes don't realize their own power and the enormity of their influence on children for good or for evil. [Much of Stanford University's Professor Linda Darling Hammond's research focuses on the impact of two "bad" teachers in back-to-back years on a student's academic preparation.] I have witnessed that for decades and it cannot be overstated. I believe that if every teacher's education program in the country devoted one course to that quote alone and used example after example of what teachers have done to destroy or uplift children, what many call the achievement gap and what I call the opportunity gap would soon disappear. Some will call this a Pollyannaish or over-simplistic solution given all of the other factors that impinge on a child's educational life (poverty, dysfunctional families, domestic violence, hunger, poor eyesight, etc.), but I would argue that it is worth a try. Much of what has been deemed "educational reform" and had billions of dollars devoted to it has failed miserably. Why not try a simple solution? The reason why this solution won't be tried is because I believe that there is no will to educate Black and Brown children at high levels in this country. There is a societal balance that requires oppressed people. Just think for a moment what would happen if all children were given the opportunity to realize their greatness. What would happen to people who work in prisons, juvenile detention centers, and jails? What would happen to the jobs of probation officers, social workers, legal defense teams, school reform organizations, and think tanks that spend millions seeking solutions to what ails poor performing students? What a sad commentary on us as human beings. That we would actually profit from the misfortune of our most vulnerable is repulsive to me and part of what has compelled me to fight valiantly for those kind of children.

Before moving on to other teachers who helped make my schooling an exception to the rule for a young Black girl growing up in the racially-charged years of the 1960's in America, I must share about that profoundly dark day in elementary school that is indelibly imprinted on my consciousness. It was November 22, 1963. I was ten years old and in the fifth grade. I have no idea who my teacher was that year, but I vividly recall her crying uncontrollably after the principal came on the intercom and announced that President John F. Kennedy had been assassinated and that school was dismissed for the day. As young children, we did not know what assassinated meant, but we were excited to get out of school early that day. It was not until we started leaving campus and saw parents driving up in tears to pick up their children that we realized that "assassinated" must have meant something terribly bad. Suddenly feeling less than jubilant about that early dismissal, we trudged home anxious to find out why everybody seemed so sad. To this day, the only reason I can give for our teacher not telling us what "assassinated" meant was because she was just too distraught. Once our parents arrived at home and our little black and white television flickered on, we started seeing images that have stayed with me all of my life. First, there was the grainy image of President Kennedy being shot and Jackie Kennedy climbing onto the trunk of the car. Then, there was the image of Jack Ruby killing Lee Harvey Oswald on live television. Most poignantly for me were the images of a riderless horse being lead down the funeral procession with its stirrups turned backwards to signify the death of its master, and of two year old, John-John saluting his fallen father at Arlington Cemetery. Ironically, in 2013, I was in DC and visited a special, 50th anniversary of the assassination exhibit at Newseum and was filled with emotion when I was transported back to that space in time while watching some of that same footage. Much later in life, I realized why that particular assassination had such a profound effect on our nation and the world. JFK and Jackie symbolized youth, vigor and new beginnings—a chance to get democracy right this time for the masses of my people who were awakening from a slumber and being summoned to demand their human rights by a young preacher named Dr. Martin Luther King, Jr.

Yes, I was a witness to much civil rights history growing up in the 1960's, but my parents had left the inner cities and moved their large family to the suburbs so that we would have opportunities that would prove ever elusive to most Black children in America. While many of our cousins languished in Watts and had front row seats when the riots erupted there, we merely watched on TV and listened to my mother's scathing commentary about those "ignorant" Black looters. Because of my mom's upbringing, she just could not understand why Blacks would destroy the very businesses that catered to them. She probably wondered where they would shop now. While we watched the conflagration from the comfort of our suburban sofa, now we realize that it was a violent response to decades of disenfranchisement and pent-up anger at an America that refused to equitably embrace the very people whose ancestors helped build this country.

By now, I was in what was called junior high (7th, 8th and 9th grades) and the only two teachers I remember during those three years were Mr. Kelly and Mrs. Albertson. Petite and red-haired, Mrs. Albertson wore pearls, a dress and high heels to class every day. She was my 8th grade Algebra teacher and the only one who ever helped me understand math well enough to get a C! She was the kind of teacher who had high expectations for all of her students and was determined to help them grasp a subject that most of us hated. While most of my students actually liked my high school English courses, I still channeled Mrs. Albertson when it came to dressing professionally and expecting the very best from all who entered my classroom. I think that the teaching profession got its first black eye when teachers decided to show up in jeans, cut-offs, flip-flops and clothes that were more appropriate for lounging around on the weekend than influencing the minds of impressionable children. While I am certainly not arguing that sloppily dressed teachers are why students don't seem to take schooling seriously, I do submit that the way a teacher dresses sends many messages to her students. How would most of us feel if we went to a doctor who wore cut-offs and flip-flops? I have had the same doctor for over 30 years and he has always greeted me with a crisp shirt, tie and tailored slacks under his white coat.

The only other teacher I remember from junior high was Mr. Kelly. Handsome and witty, all of the girls just loved him! He was my ninth grade English teacher. Because English was my favorite subject, it was a course that I naturally looked forward to. Yet, there was something magical about Mr. Kelly's class. He was such a warm and loving personality who genuinely cared about all of his students. Many years later, we heard through the grapevine that he was a gay alcoholic who died relatively young of cirrhosis of the liver. Whether or not any of that was true, he made a positive impression on me and I strived to be just like Mr. Kelly when I became a teacher. I wanted my students to love coming to my class and remember it fondly as a place of great learning, but also a space where happy laughter was frequent and encouraged. The Bible says that laughter is good medicine and I agree. I have frequented so many classrooms in the past nearly four decades where dour-faced teachers bore students to tears. Not only do they seem miserable in the profession, but they measure their success by how "hard" they come across. In order to help create joyful learners, we need joyful teachers.

While I only remember two teachers from my junior high years, I recall twice as many from my three years in high school. When I speak with Black classmates who shared my Ganesha high school experience, most still talk about how much they loved Mrs. Schneider. I am no exception. She was my junior year English teacher. More importantly, she taught Black literature and I thought I had died and gone to heaven! As I alluded to earlier, I only had White teachers from K-12 and I also attended predominantly White schools during that time period. With the benefit of many years of teaching multicultural literature and promoting culturally responsive classroom practices, I realize now that I had been steeped in Eurocentric curriculum until my junior year in high school. I have no recollection of any teaching units that highlighted the contributions of non-Whites to the world. To unabashedly promote one culture is dangerously wrong on so many levels. Not only could it lead to self-loathing for those who never learn about the greatness of their own people, but it can also serve as an incubator for White supremacy. While I am not convinced that either of these was an overt objective of the curriculum that was spoon-fed to millions of Black children beginning with the Dick and Jane books of our kindergarten and first grade years, I have seen the deleterious effects of such a narrow focus. Why would Black preschoolers prefer the White doll over the Black doll in the 1950's and in a similar study just done a few years ago, if the self-loathing was not ingrained in the psyche of those impressionable girls? Why do our teenage girls seem to have an obsession with weaves (the longer, the "prettier") and our boys seem to favor girls who wear them as opposed to girls who proudly sport "natural" hairstyles? Without belaboring this point, I hope you get my drift. When I channeled Mrs. Schneider, I celebrated the culture of all of the children in my classes. No one culture was ever exalted over others. American literature was my specialty. The novel unit was chronological and multicultural: *The Scarlet Letter, The Jungle, The Great Gatsby, Farewell to Manzanar, The Chosen, I Know Why the Caged Bird Sings*, and *House Made of Dawn*. To learn that your people's history did not begin with slavery was liberating and esteem-building. Ironically, I don't recall specific literature that Mrs. Schneider taught, but I recall how her teaching made me feel. What would our classrooms be like if all teachers cared about that?

Just as Mrs. Schneider opened up a whole new world for me through literature, Mrs. Brink did the same as my senior year English teacher. Large and melodramatic, Mrs. Brink was what many would call a "hard" teacher because she had us read books like *Cry, the Beloved Country*, which is the only novel I remember vividly of all the ones I was taught in high school. I could hardly wait to get to her class each day where I would sit rapt as she pranced around the room bringing literature to life. While I was never able to emulate Mrs. Brink's thespian skills, I did try to get my students excited about literature. Their favorite unit was usually the poetry one. After giving them a list of literary terms (e.g. simile, metaphor, personification, symbolism, etc.), I would ask them to select a favorite song that they would teach the class. Of course, it could not have any profanity, explicit sexual lyrics, or ones that denigrated people due to race, gender or sexual orientation. I will discuss that unit in more detail in another chapter.

The other two teachers who I remember most were Mr. Lahar and Mr. Wooten. Since I did not have anyone to help guide my college-prep journey, I did not take foreign language until I was a junior in high school. I chose French because my role model sister, Lilly, had studied French. Mr. Lahar was my French teacher. He had a clubfoot and walked with a serious limp. An excellent teacher who did not tolerate any misbehaving in class, Mr. Lahar was firm and fair, but not necessarily friendly. In fact, he engendered a healthy dose of fear in his students and I don't recall anyone ever crossing him. He must have actually liked me, though, because he was the advisor for the American Field Service (AFS) Club along with Mrs. Brink (who I knew loved me!) and they are the two responsible for encouraging me to apply to study abroad. I had to sit through an interview with them, then with some city-wide people before my application was selected and sent to New York for consideration. When Mr. Lahar learned that I had been selected to study in France for one year, for the first time I saw pure joy spread across his face. He was so happy for me and proud that in two short years he had given me a strong foundation in French that would help me attain fluency with relative ease. Of course, Mrs. Brink was her usual demonstrative self. She wrapped her large arms around my petite twelfth grade body and squeezed me so tight that I thought I would faint! Those were some heady days. When I wrote college letters of recommendations for students or encouraged them to try some great adventure, I was channeling Mr. Lahar and Mrs. Brink.

The fourth teacher who had an influence on me was in the social studies department. Mr. Wooten was handsome and very smart. His international relations course was taught like a college level one during my senior year. Had there been Advanced Placement or Honors courses at Ganesha, Mr. Wooten's would have been one of them. I recall that all of the smartest students in my graduating class were in there and we loved it. Even though it was the most difficult class that I took in high school, I relished the challenge and the intellectual stimulation. Frankly, there is nothing about Mr. Wooten's class that I consciously set out to emulate with my students, but it has always meant a lot to me when former students would return to visit me and say that they loved my class even though it was challenging and they might not have even earned an A or B. They talked about the rich discussions we had and how I encouraged them to think critically. That is just what I would tell Mr. Wooten if he were alive today. I think his face would light up.

Yes, they were the ones.

Chapter 3

A Golden Road: *France, Pitzer, Stanford*

On the first morning after my long-awaited arrival, I swung open the shutters and peered out the window to behold the glassy beauty of the vast Mediterranean Sea. A spectacular sunrise was unfolding just for me because I was an 18-year old Black girl from a small city in California who had been chosen to begin her post high school life in a pristine coastal sea port in Southern France. This was the beginning of a golden road traveled on toward my lifetime goal of becoming an English teacher.

Life-changing, the year in France was ushered in by a one-week orientation in New York with more than 100 other American students from around the country who had successfully weathered the highly-competitive process to become an American Field Service (AFS) scholarship recipient. Years later I learned that my parents contributed less than $250 toward the cost of that experience, yet it seemed like a fortune at a time when one gallon of gas was 29 cents. After our week in New York, we flew to France. Students going to Germany, Italy, Spain and other European countries boarded busses and headed off to one-week orientation camps before taking trains to meet their host families. Those of us in France went to Jausier and bonded. It was the summer of 1971 and some of us remain in contact to this day.

My arrival in beautiful Sete was met with much excitement. My French father, Robert Mattera, was waiting for me at the train station and had borrowed a neighbor's car to pick me up. Because he worked at the local port in an office, rode a scooter to work, and rarely ventured out of Sete, I assume that he found no need to invest in a car. I never bothered to ask about that because it simply was not important. As we meandered from the train station through the mostly-cobbled, narrow streets up to Mount St. Claire, I could hardly believe that I had actually left my close-knit (though dysfunctional) family in Pomona and my first real boyfriend (Ed Williams) to study abroad for twelve full months. From the moment I entered the home at Cite Belle Vue until I left it, I was surrounded by a kind of unconditional love that escapes most people during their lifetimes. My French mother, Celie, the heartbeat of the family, doted over me and coddled me through those fleeting moments of homesickness that year. One of the things that AFS does to try and ensure that matches work out is to find families that are slightly similar to the ones students are coming from. Since I was raised with seven sisters, I was placed in a family with five girls—Marie-Ange, Anne-Lucie, Marie-Therese, Regine and Agnes. Because all of these girls were brilliant students with sterling academic records, I was expected to do well at the lycee, too. While I did not ever achieve at their levels, I did manage to study hard enough to earn the baccalaureate certificate at the end of what would be equivalent to a 13th year of high school in the United States. Much sought-after by French high school students who choose the lycee pathway as opposed to a trade school, the bac then (as it is called in France) enabled French students to attend any university in the country, where they could gain admission, free of charge. Today, whenever I tell French people that I earned the bac, they are quite impressed. Striving for it was an expectation set early on in the Mattera household so I just did everything possible to meet that. What did I say earlier about expectations? Here we go again!

Living in France was the first major defining moment in my life. Becoming fluent in French was hastened because the English teacher at the lycee allowed me to co-teach her course from time-to-time. Also, my French family insisted that I not only use the language, but also follow the heated, highly-philosophical debates that my older French sisters would engage in with my opinionated father when they were home from college.

Marie-Ange, the oldest, was studying to become a lawyer, and Anne-Lucie, next in line, was a pre-med student. Both went on to earn their respective terminal degrees and succeed in their chosen professions. While all of the sisters were smart, I felt that the third in line, Marie-Therese, was the smartest of the bunch. She had skipped several grades, excelled in every challenging course she took in the science and math track at the lycee, graduated two years early, aced undergrad and med school, and opened her own private practice in Sete that has thrived from the onset. Since she was nearest to me in age, we became bosom buddies. If I did not do well in school, she would shake her head in disgust and my French mother would quickly reprimand her if she caught the gesture. Marie-Therese was like my personal tutor in French language and she patiently helped me find the right words to express what I needed to say. I, in turn, helped her with her English and this made us both happy. Super witty when she was not hunkered down with studying, we used to fill the house with laughter.

The Mattera household had much love to go around. My French mother's aunt (Tante Adele) lived with us and cared for a developmentally delayed adult cousin, Emile, who I was scared of for the first few weeks of my stay because his twisted legs caused him to lumber when he walked, he was cross-eyed and had slurred speech. Once I got over my fear, we bonded and he loved to engage me in "conversations" that were usually nonsensical. I played along and he delighted in that. Rounding out the extended family were Maman and Papa—elderly parents of my French mother. Quite large and always brooding, Maman lumbered around the house keeping herself busy and out of the way. Although Papa was blind, he was always in a good mood and dispensed great wisdom. Born and raised in Algeria, he reluctantly moved his family to Southern France after Algeria won its independence. Fluent in Arabic (like Maman), he spoke fondly of his life there. I loved to be in his presence. Although my mother, Papa and Maman are all now deceased, my father still lives in the spacious, multi-story condo that they filled with so many beautiful memories for me. The five sisters purchased and remodeled a house in that same building and use it as a vacation space whenever they all come together with their own husbands and children.

Returning to the United States from France was a mixed blessing. Allow me to back up for a minute.

Because my mother was a cook and my stepfather was a janitor, they knew nothing about how to help their children prepare, enroll and succeed in college. What they did know was that college was an option we should pursue so during my senior year of high school, I applied to my top three schools—Pitzer College (part of the Claremont Colleges consortium), Long Beach State and San Jose State. Let me interject here that I did not even know that Historically Black Colleges and Universities (HBCUs) existed and if my White high school counselors knew, they never once mentioned them to me. I am not even suggesting that I might have considered attending one of them, but I do think there is value in HBCUs and believe that students should have options when it comes to college choices. As a teacher, counselor and project coordinator, I always told my Black students about HBCUs. A number of them chose to attend and had excellent experiences. Many years after my graduation from college, my only child would choose to attend Spelman, a top-ranking HBCU for women, and have such a remarkable experience that it continues to touch her life even today.

Receiving the "fat" envelope offering admission from each of my three colleges the spring of my senior year was thrilling indeed, even though I knew that I would have to defer enrollment while I studied in France. While I was in France, I asked my parents to fill out the financial aid papers. Because they missed the deadlines (who knows what crisis they were dealing with when it approached), I did not have the funds to attend any of those schools. Instead, I enrolled at a local community college, Mt. San Antonio, and earned a two-year degree in English before transferring to Pitzer. Although initially disappointed that I could not enroll immediately into Pitzer (my first choice school), going to Mt. Sac was a blessing in disguise. Not only did I have to pay much less for my first two years of undergraduate school than I would have had to pay at Pitzer, I was still dreaming in French when I returned so I needed to ease myself into a college routine and get that year abroad out of my system. Because of my own positive experience in a community college setting, I have always encouraged "late bloomers" or students who could not afford a four-year institution to take advantage of that option. Unfortunately, too many students get comfortable at community colleges and never earn enough credits to transfer. I also counsel my students about avoiding that trap.

Enrolling at Pitzer felt like a dream come true. The youngest of the Claremont Colleges, Pitzer was the perfect place for me to grow intellectually and mature as a young woman well on her way to realizing Mr. Stevenson's goal for my life. Since Pitzer is part of a robust consortium of colleges that included Claremont Men's (now Claremont McKenna), Scripps, Pomona and Harvey Mudd, I had the great privilege of being able to take courses on any of those other campuses. Because I was still fluent in French, I took advanced courses like French Literature of the Colonized. It was at the Claremont Colleges that I fell in love for the first time with *Things Fall Apart* and *No Longer at Ease* by the brilliant, award-winning Nigerian author—Chinua Achebe. Although I had some incredibly amazing professors, Dr. Agnes Jackson is the one I simply adored. Regal, fiercely proud of her Blackness, dauntingly difficult and no-nonsense, she taught a course entitled Black Women Fiction Writers and my parched intellect could not get enough of books like *The Bluest Eye, Sula*, and *I Know Why the Caged Bird Sings*. Glory had nothing on that experience. It was severe Dr. Jackson who told me that while I was a very good writer, if I wanted to be the very best of English teachers, I needed to take a grammar course. I was stunned! I had already successfully completed three years of English courses and earned A's in each one, yet she was the first professor to tell me that my writing needed touching up. Once she heard that I had been accepted into Stanford University's Teacher Education Program, Dr. Jackson reminded me not to get in front of students until I polished my grammar. I lost no time enrolling in a grammar course at a local community college during the second semester of my senior year at Pitzer and I am so glad that I did. Not only did my writing improve, I was able to explain grammatical concepts with ease when I did finally get my own students. Sometimes critical advice hurts. Rather than ignore it, we need to turn it over a few times and see what value it really has. More often than not, it will be absolutely for our best.

Armed with a good grasp of grammar, I graduated from Pitzer in June of 1976, and two weeks later I was living in Wilbur dormitory on the Stanford University campus studying to earn a master's in education and lifetime teaching credentials in English, French and psychology. I was also a few weeks pregnant by choice. For almost three years, I had been in a tumultuous relationship with the second love of my life. Without going into too many sordid details, the relationship was rocky at best when I received my Stanford acceptance packet. Realizing that it would surely not survive once I moved to Northern California, I made the conscious decision to have a baby by George Sweed. Telling him about this solo decision and having to live with his sense of outrage and betrayal were the lowest points in my life at that time. In spite of the emotional pain, I plunged into graduate school and earned stellar grades. When I gave birth to Alicia D'Ann Sweed on February 1, 1977, the Dean of Stanford's School of Education and his wife were my first visitors at Stanford Hospital and were followed by a steady stream of students in my STEP cohort who showered me and the baby with unconditional love. Although George and I had stayed in communication throughout most of the pregnancy, the relationship was clearly over and we were both content to move on with our respective lives. Because I had always been the obedient child who was careful not to cause my parents any grief and who took pride in being the honor student praised for her great choices, it was very difficult to tell my mother about this pregnancy. Having just endured a brutally bitter divorce from my stepfather, my mother just did not deserve more heartbreak and disappointment. When I finally found the courage to tell her, she just sighed and said she knew that one of her girls was pregnant because she had been dreaming of fish. I was so relieved, and assured her that I would still graduate that June with my cohort. I kept my promise and she showed up just as proud as she had been a year earlier when she and my birth father celebrated my graduation from Pitzer.

While now I do not think it is wise for a woman to make a unilateral decision to get pregnant without the benefit of a solid marriage, giving birth to Alicia was the greatest joy of my life and changed it forever.

Religion had never played a major role in our lives. My mother had been forced to attend church six out of seven days each week when she was a little girl and decided that she would not subject her children to that. My birth father was raised Seventh-day Adventist, but left the church when he was in his late teens and never returned. When he married my mother, he wanted nothing to do with the church of his childhood. Yet his mother was a devout Seventh-day Adventist who showed my mother so much love and tenderness, especially when my father was at his abusive worse, so we were often allowed to go to church with our paternal grandmother as young children. In fact, my mother loved my grandmother so much that she gave me her middle name—Irene. I wore it like a badge of honor.

Only one of my grandmother's 14 children stayed in the Seventh-day Adventist Church throughout her lifetime and that was Aunt Alice. When Candace, the sister one year older than me, graduated from Cal Poly Pomona, she went to live in San Diego with that aunt.

Soon after, Candace was baptized into the Seventh-day Adventist Church. As a result of some traumatic personal events in her life, Candace came to live with me while I was enrolled at Stanford. She started attending the Adventist Church in Mountain View where I lived and encouraged me to join her. I finally relented at eight months pregnant and attended a communion service. Still full of shame for being an unwed mother, it was liberating to hear that I could start my life over as a new creature in Christ Jesus. Wanting a new life for me and a bright beginning for Alicia, I was baptized into the Adventist church when she was about six weeks old.

Although my grandmother died one month before I was baptized, I enthusiastically embraced my new religion and have been an active leader in the same church for more than 38 years. My mother used to always say that my grandmother would be so proud of that. Given the fact that Alicia has followed in my footsteps and is also active in her local Adventist Church is a great source of pride for me. To God be the glory!

When I consider the many opportunities I was offered, from a year of study in France to a rich education at Pitzer and Stanford, I realize that not many Black young people are so fortunate. My pathway was, indeed, golden and it prepared me to step into the career that roly-poly Mr. Stevenson envisioned for a little Black girl who showed some talent in writing. **I will say it again.**

The power of a teacher's influence for good or evil cannot be overstated.

Chapter 4

One Career. One School District.

Jostling with Harvard and Teacher's College at Columbia University for the nation's spot as the number one School of Education, Stanford's Teacher Education Program (STEP) fell short of my expectations when it came to preparing me for what English teachers spend the bulk of their time doing (grading papers) and about five years after graduating I went back and told them so. They suggested that I come and teach their students how to tackle that dreadful task more efficiently. Candidly, I told them that I was too busy grading papers when I was not in the actual classroom!

Nonetheless, Stanford's name absolutely provides access and I am sure it helped me land the first teaching job in the only school district where I would ever work during my 35 years in the profession. Spanning 103 acres of prime Silicon Valley real estate, Independence High School opened in the fall of 1976 as the first new high school in Santa Clara County in several decades and that is where my career began as an English teacher. The vision of the legendary superintendent Frank Fiscalini, of the East Side Union High School District (ESUHSD), Independence boasted a public library, planetarium, Olympic-size pool and a lap pool, two gymnasiums and enough classrooms to accommodate 5,000 students with ease. It boasted a wing of state-of-the-art "shop" classes that included plastics, automotive repair, wood and metal. During my tenure there, it even had a gourmet restaurant at one point. The delicious meals were prepared by students under the watchful eye of a trained chef. Divided into five "villas" of 1,000 students each with its own principal and cadre of core teachers, I was assigned to Bicentennial Hall after successfully interviewing with the dashing and gregarious principal, Guy Klitgaard, and the warm and intelligent English department chair, Barbara Gillespie. Both were always there to ensure that I had everything I needed to succeed as a teacher, and I thrived under their leadership.

Recalling my own active high school career, I plunged right into club sponsorships. Linda Flournoy and I were in the same program at Stanford and were both hired to begin teaching at Independence in the fall of 1977. Dorothy Hines had already been teaching in the district a few years before us. As Black teachers, we felt a responsibility to help students who looked like us to succeed in high school so we started the first Black Student Union (BSU) at Independence and would serve as advisors for the next ten years. Eschewing the sponsorship of dances and talent shows, we wanted our students to learn about their history and gain pride in being Black. Dorothy owned a veritable museum of historical artifacts, art, pictures and magazines. Every February, we would organize Black History Month presentations featuring a great deal of these treasures and teachers would look forward to the opportunity to bring their classes because they could always count on high-quality educational experiences. As BSU advisors, we also took our students on field trips and to leadership conferences sponsored by the United Black Student Unions of California (UBSUC). Sadly, those days are long gone and many Black students rarely have culturally-affirming experiences on the campuses in the ESUHSD nor throughout this country. I maintain that part of why Black and Brown students tend to underperform even in affluent Silicon Valley schools is because they don't feel cared about and valued. While I never met a teacher who went into the profession to damage these students, it happens every day due in large part to what has been termed unconscious bias. Unpacking the phrase, it simply is a teacher unconsciously treating certain students with less regard because of his or her own upbringing. Negative images of Black and Brown people are stored in the subconscious and resurrected in school settings when a teacher decides who to call on in class, how to respond to a perceived threat, who to recommend for Honors or

Advanced Placement and in countless other ways. Only through specialized training can teachers begin to understand their own inherent biases and seek to consciously keep them in check when they are dealing with impressionable children entrusted in their care. In my career, I knew precious few teachers who were willing to become this introspective about themselves and their craft. Most assumed defensive postures or merely tried to blame "those" kids. Let me mention here that non-White teachers are often just as guilty as White ones. In fact, that internalized racism is often more insidious because the Black or Brown student will "assume" that a teacher who looks like him would not harbor such biases. Until there is a dramatic shift in how teachers are prepared in schools of education around this country, these issues and related others will continue to serve as obstacles to the academic success of the masses of Black and Brown students. A few, like me, will always manage to successfully navigate the system. Why can't we be the rule and not the exception?

In addition to my sponsorship of the BSU, I also created several other clubs and served as the advisor. Because I taught primarily college-prep juniors and seniors for the first 14 years of my career at Independence and had always been interested in international relations since the days of Mr. Wooten's high school course on that topic, I started a Model United Nations club with some very bright students who excelled in school. For ten years,

I helped them prepare to become delegates representing some countries I had scarcely heard of and well-known ones, and chaperoned their annual overnight trips to UC Berkeley where they argued before the General Assembly and always made me proud. For those students not disciplined enough for the rigors of the MUN, I also founded Sunrays; a multicultural club designed to bring together the many different ethnic groups that made up Independence's student body. It also thrived.

As I reflect on my life, I realize that there is a theme that runs through it—the importance of lasting relationships. In spite of the drama and trauma that characterized my growing up years, relationships were always central to our family life. While I was still an undergraduate, I created a YWCA club called Essence of Beauty for Black high school girls. To this day, I can't recall how I stumbled upon this opportunity, but I remember wanting to help the girls navigate high school successfully and enroll in college. Again, the idea of building a lasting relationship was central to the design of that program. Thus, when the opportunity arose early in my career at Independence to work in the Electronics Academy as the charter English teacher, I embraced it wholeheartedly because it meant that I would stay with a cohort of freshmen until they graduated from high school. While many of my colleagues thought I was crazy to want to teach the same students for four years, I loved the idea to build trusting relationships and ensure that the cohort had the English skills necessary to either enter college or find gainful employment right after high school. In addition to my role as the English teacher, I had counterparts in math, science and electronics. If students advanced beyond the subjects that we taught, they were free to take courses outside of the Academy. Inspired by a newspaper article about a history teacher who helped his students write a novel based on the Michener style of historical fiction, I sought to do the same with my cohort beginning in their sophomore year. After an overnight trip to Madera (about two hours from San Jose) to meet the teacher and his students, we came back fired up to write our own book based on the land where Independence was located. Each of my four classes of students was assigned a century to research—1600's, 1700's, 1800's and 1900's. Little did I know that this would become the most difficult project I had ever undertaken with high school students. What was supposed to take one school year to complete, took three! I had to essentially pull all of the research together myself so that the book would be coherent. It was finally published in the cohort's senior year and I was one relieved teacher. After my students graduated, I was ready to move on to the next exciting teaching assignment and there was a whole group of English teachers who vied for my job. I guess they finally saw the power of the model.

Since I am musing about relationships, this is probably a good place to interject a little bit about what was going on in my personal life along those lines as my teaching career progressed. Although my birth father did not help raise us, my mother and stepfather ensured that we visited with him and his parents often. They were always important parts of our lives and it was my father who gave me away in April of 1979 when I married the man who would become my husband for the next 18 years. I met John Watkins when I was the youth leader at my church in East Palo Alto and he was an electrical engineering major at nearby Stanford University who attended my church from time to time. Painfully shy and introverted, John had never even had a girlfriend before we started dating, got engaged and married over a two-year period. Brilliant and witty, John accepted Alicia as his own daughter and was a good father. John used to say that opposites attract and then they repel. That is what happened to us. Averse to revealing sordid details about my life and other people, suffice it to say that though my divorce was very painful, it really was for the best. After John graduated from Stanford, he went on to work for Hewlett-Packard and was wooed with stock options to work for a relatively new start-up called Sun Microsystems. The decision to join Sun's staff resulted in financial benefits for our family. Therefore, when my divorce was final in July 1996, I had the financial freedom to spread my wings and take on projects that would help thousands of students and their families throughout the state of California and eventually the country. Before I launch into all of that, let me just step back and talk about what happened after I left the Electronics Academy.

I languished in the "traditional" classroom for one year while scanning around for something new and different to do in teaching. I read about an alternative school that was going to open on the Independence campus and applied for one of the positions. Pegasus was one of several "small-but-necessary" schools in the ESUHSD slated to open that year. It was for 11th and 12th grade students who had fallen behind on their credits and needed to catch up in order to graduate from high school. There was a morning session of merely three and a half hours and an afternoon session of the same duration. Three morning and three afternoon teachers collaborated on the curriculum which was theme-based. We had our own principal, secretary, and counselor. The vast majority of the students thrived in this alternative setting and graduated with high school diplomas. I taught at Pegasus for eight years and loved every moment. Again, this idea of lasting relationships was foundational at Pegasus. Why did these students thrive in this setting and not in traditional school? They had a small team of professionals who were thrilled that they wanted a second chance at high school and were willing to put in all of the extra work. We made that plain to them and were there to scaffold their success. While I realize that most teachers don't have the luxury of only having 60 students on a daily basis like I had at Pegasus, most don't have that many who are gang-affiliated, drug users, pregnant or parenting moms or saddled with any number of problems either. Teachers need to stop making excuses for not being able to successfully engage so many of our Black and Brown students. About five years into my teaching career, it dawned on me that very few Black students were making it into my college-prep English courses. Fortunately, there was an organization called Black Educators of East Side (BEES) and I was a member. At about that time, the BEES decided to join with the Black Educators of Alum Rock School District (BEARS) to create a new organization that could yield more influence in Silicon Valley. I was one of the founding members of the Santa Clara County Alliance of Black Educators (SCCABE) about thirty years ago. It is an affiliate of the National Alliance of Black School Educators (NABSE). We host an annual Back-to-School social so that area educators can mingle and listen to some well-known keynote speakers or distinguished panelists. For decades, we have honored Black students transitioning from 5th/6th, 8th or 12th grade at a ceremony that annually attracts hundreds of parents and community members. We have hosted Kwanzaa events and weighed in on county-wide issues that affect Black students. There are more details about the SCCABE in chapter 7.

When I became president of the SCCABE in 1994, I was always looking for more ways to extend our influence. When I was approached by two men (Halim Mustafa and

Rasheed Salaam) from an organization called The Healing Institute about partnering with them to establish science fairs in honor of Dr. George Washington Carver, I was intrigued with that idea since so many of our children were not going into STEM (science, technology, engineering, math) fields. After convincing my board to give it a try, I worked with Halim and Rasheed to create the Dr. George Washington Carver Scholars Program (CSP). The CSP was extremely successful for three years. Due to differences between me and Halim and Rasheed about how to best grow the CSP, I quit the partnership.

A few years before the CSP, I had been working with other NABSE affiliates in the Bay Area to establish a state-wide organization to address my growing concerns about what was happening to Black children beyond Silicon Valley. After resigning as coordinator of the CSP in January 2001, we officially launched the California Alliance of African American Educators (CAAAE) in August of that same year. There is more about the CAAAE in chapter 7.

Parents who had been in the CSP approached me about creating another STEM program. Still smarting from the acrimony created as a result of my decision to leave the CSP, I was reluctant to start another one. Finally, the parents prevailed and I launched the Dr. Frank S. Greene Scholars Program (GSP) at the same time that the CAAAE was born. Named after an African American scientist who made his fortune in Silicon Valley and helped pave the way for today's computers, the GSP has been extremely successful. We send 100% of our students to college, 90% graduate in four years with a BA or BS degree and about 60% of those degrees are in STEM fields. That is more than five times the national average of African American students earning STEM degrees. For ten years, we were the only all-African American MESA (Mathematics Engineering Science Achievement) chapter in the state of California. As MESA began to experience serious financial distress and started cutting back on its offerings, we decided to end what had been a great partnership and become an active chapter of the National Society of Black Engineers (NSBE).

When I was coordinating the CSP, we cultivated a relationship with Dr. T.J. Rodgers, the brilliant founder and CEO of Cypress Semiconductor. I like to tell the story of how I first met T.J. He was on a panel focused on diversifying the pipeline of STEM professionals in Silicon Valley. T. J. is what many call a maverick in the valley and he marches to his own drum. He is a CEO who is often chided for hiring so many foreigners to work at his company on HB1 visas. On the panel with him and others was the dean of the School of Engineering at the University of California at Davis. He attempted to publicly chastise T.J. by stating that if Cypress did not hire so many foreigners, his graduates would not have such a hard time getting jobs. T.J. did not skip a beat and said, "If your engineering school was not 18th in the nation, maybe I would hire your graduates!" T.J. had done his research and the school was 18th. I was too far from the panelists to see just how flushed that dean's face was, but I think the moderator quickly intervened and changed the subject. During the Q&A, I went to the microphone and announced that the CSP had just received its first $50,000 from Intel and that if any company reps were serious about diversifying the pipeline, I would be in the back of the room and happy to talk with them. When the session was over, an Intel vice president ran up to me and thanked me for making the announcement about her company's donation. I had no idea that anyone from Intel was even in the room. Soon, there was a line of people waiting to discuss ways their companies could partner with us. That is how I got the first group of funders for the CSP apart from Intel. The way we got Intel in the first place was because I had written an article in the SCCABE's newsletter about our new partnership with The Healing Institute to run a STEM program. Intel's regional education director, Julie Dunkle, read the article and called me. For months we worked on a proposal that she felt Intel's foundation would fund and that is how we got that first $50,000. Intel's support was so amazing from the start that we named the program the Intel Carver Scholars Program (ICSP). At its height, we had about 154 students in grades K-12 and each Scholar had a water-falled laptop from Intel with a brand new operating system and Microsoft suite. Intel also provided free technical training for the Scholars and their parents. We were featured in their company newsletters and in a video about the company's philanthropy.

After my line was finished, I got in T.J.'s line. When it was my turn I launched into my spiel about the CSP and he said, "You are the one who just got $50,000 from Intel, right?" I nodded. He said, "My company (Cypress Semiconductor) is half that size. Call my office tomorrow and I will give you $25,000." No kidding! Trembling with disbelief, somehow I made it to my car and quickly dialed Rasheed to tell him the amazing news. I called the office the next day and in two weeks we had our first check of $25,000. At that year's first science fair gala with about 600 attendees and a boat-load of corporate sponsorships, we asked T.J. to introduce the keynote speaker. The next year, T.J. donated another $25,000 and we asked him to keynote the gala that had grown to about 800 attendees. In the third year, the $25,000 donation was made and ten Cypress executives and their spouses were in attendance along with about 1,100 other people.

After I ceased involvement with the ICSP and it closed its doors, I sought to continue the very powerful partnership that we had started with Dr. Rodgers. A great champion of the GSP from its onset, we would not have half the successes that we have garnered had it not been for the unwavering support of T.J. By the way, he is a White man.

When the CAAAE's new board chairman, Henry Taylor (a highly-competent, professional fundraising executive) took the helm, one of the first things he said is that we need to go to our most consistent donors and ask for more support. T.J. was the first person who came to mind. We prepared a PowerPoint presentation outlining my vision for the CAAAE, but we were actually there to ask if we could use his winery for our board retreat. I forgot to mention that T.J. owns several spectacular wineries and is also a gourmet cook. Anyway, the first item on my list was a computer lab for the Scholars and office space for the CAAAE and its future staff. T.J. stopped me there and asked how many computers we would need. I glanced at my chairman because we had not anticipated that question. You must be ready when opportunity knocks! I casually said, "Oh, 30 computers would be fine." T.J. said, "I can do that. What's next on your list?" Trying hard not to look astonished, I continued with the rest of the list. When we finally got to the "ask" for retreat space, T.J. got up from his seat and walked over to a picture hanging on the wall in his office and said that this was his winery and it was still under construction. He then went on to offer his own conference space stating that it rivals any hotel in the area. That was in June. By the time the retreat took place in August, we had a fully-furnished computer lab with 30 networked laptops, a laser printer and office space for me and three future employees. That was 1,840 square feet of prime Silicon Valley real estate at Cypress' headquarters in San Jose!

In the beginning of its existence, the CAAAE's board was quite large. It consisted of two coordinators from each of the five original regions (10 people) plus a president, vice president, secretary and treasurer. For that year's retreat, we also invited about five other Advisory Board members. I had asked T.J. to share with the board on Friday's opening night how he built Cypress into a Fortune 1000 company and what lessons we could learn as we were growing the CAAAE. Not only did he do a fantastic job of sharing, before his address, he hosted a wine and cheese reception, and a gourmet dinner replete with china, silver and tablecloths. He had lunch catered on Saturday and elegantly packaged lunches to go on Sunday. He gifted each one of us with a Cypress polo shirt celebrating its 25th anniversary, his book entitled No Excuses Management, and Jim Collins' best-seller, Good to Great (in which Cypress is mentioned). Is that a first-class benefactor or what?!

You might be wondering why I spent so much time writing about the CAAAE's work in a chapter devoted to my tenure in one school district. All of this was happening while I was also still employed in various capacities by the ESUHSD. I coordinated the CAAAE after hours so to speak. As the CAAAE began to grow by leaps and bounds and the GSP was becoming more demanding as well, I realized that I could not continue doing both. I approached the ESUHSD's superintendent at the time, the affable Bob Nunez, and asked if the CAAAE could enter into an agreement that would allow me to remain on the district's payroll while working full-time for the CAAAE. The plan was that the CAAAE would reimburse the district for my salary. Because Bob had knowledge of my work with the CAAAE and GSP, he agreed. For the next three years, I ran the CAAAE full-time. During the second year of that arrangement, I learned about the AT&T Foundation's Aspire High School Success grant competition. I resurrected Project WORD (Working On Re-defining our Destiny), embellished it and added the component of staying with all 41 of the African American freshmen at Oak Grove in the ESUHSD until they graduated from high school. I submitted the grant on behalf of the ESUHSD and the CAAAE. We won the largest grant offered ($100,000 per year for four years). The journey with those students forms the basis for the next chapter of this book. I think you will like the ride.

Chapter 5

A Few Bumps Along the Way

After working in the same school district for 35 years as a teacher, counselor, and project director, I understand more fully why my brother did not do well in school and was ultimately expelled in 10th grade for throwing a chair at a White teacher who called him the "n" word. He dropped out and never returned to high school. My brother was not unlike the thousands of Black boys who are considered "oppositional" students—those who challenge the status quo and usually end up in the principal's office even though many are very bright with great promise.

The only one of my nine siblings who never graduated from high school, my brother was brutally murdered at age 24. My brother was born prematurely so for 24 days, we were the same age. Growing up, I hated that because people used to call us twins. I did not want a boy for a twin! Years later, we became super close and I loved him deeply. His life was a casebook example of the school-to-prison pipeline. While he was in and out of jail for petty crimes, he never went to prison. Ironically, at the time of his death, he was turning his life around. I was so devastated by his murder that for ten years I never spoke about it. While pursuing my second master's degree in counseling, I was asked to write a "twilight journal" to say goodbye to someone who had left my life abruptly. It was just the cathartic release that I needed.

Henry (who we called brotha') was spoiled rotten as a child. I believe his problems began the moment he started kindergarten. He was always getting in trouble. Although he was very intelligent, he soon started to hate school. While I am not aware of what happened in those predominantly White classrooms where my brother was often one of the only Black students, I assume that he did not find a "friendly" array of teachers who took the time to understand that he was not a "bad" boy. He was just accustomed to getting his way. My brother was a poet who loved his parents and siblings. I often wonder what his life trajectory would have been if even one teacher had embraced his genius and nurtured his soul. I think it was my brother's tragic death that fueled within me the desire to be that teacher for students who were trying to make their way through the vagaries of life. Project WORD was just the vehicle for doing that.

Project WORD was the highlight of my career in the ESUHSD. In order to provide the superintendent with an extra incentive to allow me to run the CAAAE full-time, I offered to shepherd all of the Black freshmen at Oak Grove High School to graduation in four years. He thought that was a great idea so in the fall of 2007, I started working with 41 students and no real budget. Fortunately, the Alpha Phi Alpha fraternity had already been on campus for a few years as volunteer tutors so I partnered with them to build a more robust program to serve the targeted freshmen. The unwavering support of four men (Wilbur Jackson, Bill Nettles, Harold Clay and Bill Boone) associated with that fraternity was so important to Project WORD's ultimate success that I allowed two of them to write the next chapter in this book from their perspective.

There were 22 boys and 19 girls in the original cohort. Two girls were high-achievers (3.5 grade point average or above), but the majority of the students scored average or below average grades. Their home environments varied from stable mother and father present and involved to parents in prison or jail or on drugs. Contrary to popular belief, every parent in the program cared about his or her child's success in school. Unfortunately, many were so consumed with working, keeping shelter and food for the family, or dealing with serious health challenges that they often were not able to support their children as they would have liked to.

Project WORD came into existence when Joe Coto first became the superintendent of the ESUHSD. He paid several Black administrators and teachers to convene for one week with his right hand staffer, Lorraine Guerin, in what he called a Productivity College. He did the same with some Latino staff members. During that week, we discussed the problems facing Black students and keeping them from realizing their true potential. More importantly, we came up with ideas that could help us address these issues. Unfortunately, we were given no budget to implement these ideas. Some of us tried to at least "mentor" a few students on our various campuses, but this fizzled out after the first year because there were so many other demands competing for our time. Project WORD was dormant until 1997 when I convinced Superintendent Coto to allow me to run it full time. Again, because of my track record of success working with Black students and my stature as a teacher, he allowed me to pilot Project WORD. I chose Yerba Buena High School because it had one of the few Black principals in the district—Julia Lawrence. I had worked closely with Julia on projects associated with the SCCABE.

There were 81 Black students at Yerba Buena when I launched Project WORD and I was committed to helping each one of them achieve academic and social success. I used a number of approaches to supporting the students, including: incentives for good grades; motivational t-shirts, posters, bookmarks, Black history calendars; field trips to local colleges; leadership training through the UBSUC; regular contact with parents of students who were not maintaining a C average or better;

and regular contact with teachers of students who were earning less than C grades. Project WORD was very successful and even credited with helping one Black student, Didi Mwengela, enroll at Stanford on a partial scholarship. Didi did very well at Stanford, went to medical school and, the last I heard, is a successful physician. On the other end of the spectrum, I enrolled the lowest performing students in a study skills course. Many of those students were bright and just needed some pushing and nurturing. In fact, I ran into one of them about one year ago when I was making a deposit at a Chase Bank branch. At 28 years old, he is now a Private Client Banker helping wealthy customers manage their assets. It was a joyful reunion and he thanked me for never giving up on him. Is that not what teachers are supposed to do?

After Project WORD had been at Yerba Buena for one and half years, Julia left and Dan Moser became the principal. He allowed me to finish off that school year because he "inherited" Project WORD. However, at the end of that year, he told me that he wanted me back in the classroom to teach English full time. By then, I had seen first-hand how Black students could succeed if closely monitored by a caring adult so I told him that I wanted to continue with Project WORD instead. He told me that it was not an option. I appealed to Superintendent Coto to intervene, but he chose not to interfere with his principal's decision. I had no job! The tiny Black community in San Jose was outraged. About 100 Black community members showed up at a board meeting and demanded that the district find me a job that would use my talents and passion for helping Black students. It would take that kind of pressure and about two months of my threatening to go out on stress leave before I finally ended up with a position that I loved.

By then, I had helped start the Intel Carver Scholars Program (ICSP) so Superintendent Coto allowed me to run it full time for the remainder of that school year while I stayed on the district's payroll. Although I still longed to run Project WORD, I was most grateful for the opportunity to focus on the ICSP.

At the end of that school year, I applied for a job as Director of Silicon Valley Service for a small school reform organization in San Francisco called Partners in School Innovation. After being offered that job, I took a leave of absence from my district. Working for Partners was a wonderful experience. I was responsible for coaching three principals (Julie Pacheco, Susan Wright, and Janice Hobbs) at Edenvale, Stipe and Grant elementary schools respectively in San Jose, and overseeing very competent AmeriCorps workers who supported the teachers as they implemented the reform that was designed to help close academic gaps for students in those predominantly Latino schools. At the end of the first year of working for Partners, our executive director (Jeremy Singer) dropped a bombshell on us one day and announced that he was quitting and moving back to New York. This sent shockwaves through the organization and caused a crisis for me. I had been hired at the same time as my counterpart who will remain nameless in this book. With Jeremy stepping down, the board had decided to hire my counterpart and told me that I would now have to do my job and hers! When I said that I would not, I was told that there was no other job for me at Partners. I was stunned and angry that I would be let go in such a callous manner. I appealed to the founder of Partners (Julian Phillips) and that fell on deaf ears. I had developed a very close bond with most of the AmeriCorps workers at Partners. When they found out how I was treated, many of them expressed sadness and even anger. Soon after my departure, two other key staffers left Partners as well— Dr. Ida Oberman and Brian Gadsen. The organization went through a tumultuous time. I could say much more, but why bash?

By then it was September and my district had done all of its hiring for that year. I lived off of my severance package for about two months, then landed a consulting job. If my close friend, Jewel Johnson, had not helped me refinance my home (which had considerable equity in it) through a company she was working for at the time, I would have been in serious financial trouble because consulting jobs were few and far between.

Because I was tenured, I was able to return to my district the next school year and select the school where I wanted to teach. I chose the first brand new high school in Silicon Valley since Independence had opened in 1976—Evergreen Valley—because one of my favorite colleagues, Tim McDonough, was the principal. Tim and I had worked in the English department at Independence many years earlier and when he was the founding principal of Pegasus and I admired his leadership. While it was great to work with Tim again and I had a "dream" schedule (five college-prep English courses), I missed the students like those I had taught at Pegasus. The next year, there was an opening at Phoenix (a school like Pegasus) and I happily joined that staff.

For the next two years, I had the privilege of working with Merle Boxill—a gifted science teacher who got her start in the district because I had recommended her many years earlier. Merle is from St. Lucia and she had immigrated to the United States with her husband to pursue masters degrees at Stanford University. Their brilliant oldest daughter (Diane) had been the roommate of one of my "adopted" daughters (Lenore Joseph) when they were both freshmen at Stanford. Unfortunately, Diane had to drop out of Stanford because she could not garner enough financial aid to cover all of her expenses. A gifted seamstress and pianist, she opened a business close to Stanford using both talents. My daughter was soon one of her piano students. Diane knew that I was a teacher so one day she told me that her mother could not find a job as a high school science teacher and could I help her. I called my close friend and colleague, Frances Higashi Renteria, who was in charge of Human Resources in our district at the time. Within weeks, Merle had a job! She went on to have an illustrious career in the district, was an administrator at Evergreen Valley High School for a while, then chose to finish off her career working at Phoenix. We had countless, rich conversations about what ails American education and what should be done to "fix" it. When I landed the AT&T grant to run Project WORD full-time, I left Phoenix. The happiest news here is that Diane went back to Stanford after many years and earned her undergraduate degree. I was honored to be in attendance at her Black Graduation Ceremony in Stanford's cavernous Memorial Auditorium, which was nearly filled to capacity with proud parents and beaming friends and relatives of the class of 2014. The icing on the cake is that I was re-united with my "adopted" daughter, Lenore, and her sister, Sharon who came from the East Coast to celebrate Diane's graduation. Both of these brilliant, self-effacing Black women have successful careers as physicians. What wonderful role models are they for Black girls everywhere!

Two years before I retired, I was required to teach two English courses to augment the AT&T grant. I was, once again, able to select the school where I would teach. I chose Silver Creek High because another colleague who I admired, Thelma Boac, was the principal. Having been away from the "traditional" classroom for so long, I actually relished my time ending my career as I had started. I was assigned two freshmen, college-prep courses and I was able to use some of the best lessons I had ever created and the students seemed to love them. Their favorite lesson (and mine!) was from the poetry unit. In chapter 3 of this book, I stated that I would share about that lesson in more detail. You might recall that students had to select a favorite song. It could not contain profanity nor derogatory lyrics about women, men, sexual orientation, or race. Each student had to type the lyrics or print them so that I could put them on a transparency, which they shared with the class when they "taught" the song. Before they ever played the music, they had to identify at least two literary terms that were in the lyrics and explain how they related to the definitions. They also had to summarize the main message of the song. After they played the music, they had to tell how the music affected the lyrics. Because I only listen to oldies and gospel, for the first time I heard artists like Lupe Fiasco, Tupac, Katie Perry, Taylor Swift and Justin Bieber. While the presentations were taking place, my students had to take notes. After each one was finished, they also had to submit brief feedback ranging from eye contact to posture. Although getting through up to 30 presentations of about 5-7 minutes each took a great deal of time, the variety of music kept students engaged. The unit ended with a test on the presentations. That was when it was evident who took great notes and who did not. Even though they could not use their notes during the test, they were expected to study from them. Once the presentations were finished, we started studying famous poets and poems and it was gratifying to see how easily the vast majority of the students could correctly identify the literary terms therein. There are so many ways to make subjects come alive for students. Because I always taught 90 minutes from what is called Steinbeck country, for years I did a unit on that author, students raised money and we would spend an entire day visiting that region—from his birthplace in Salinas to Cannery Row in Monterey.

So we have come full circle on this part of my journey. Although bumpy at times, it was still an amazing ride.

Chapter 6

Project WORD

Alpha Phi Alpha Fraternity, Inc., is dedicated to academic excellence as stated in its mission statement: "Alpha Phi Alpha Fraternity, Inc., develops leaders, promotes brotherhood, and academic excellence, while providing service and advocacy to its communities." Since its founding in 1906 at Cornell University in Ithaca, New York, members have engaged in advancing the state of African American people. This drive led to the introduction of the "Go to High School Go to College" program in the 1920s. This program has been continuously improved to the curriculum currently delivered by its 700 chapters, both college and alumni.

The Silicon Valley chapter, Eta Sigma Lambda, initiated its support in 2006 of Oak Grove High School when Chapter President Charles Jones met with Principal Richard Frias offering a volunteer-based, after school program specifically for African American students. This effort evolved over the next couple of years until a partnership with the California Alliance of African Educators was formed in 2008 - 2009. The "Go to High School Go to College" curriculum was used to enrich the academic experience while motivating the students to graduate on time and maximize their performance. This partnership with the CAAAE's Project WORD was a natural alliance as the goals meshed very well.

The fraternity provided guest lecturers who covered the following topics:

- **African American History and Contributions to American Society**
- **Conflict Resolution**
- **Career Planning**
- **Study Skills**
- **Team Building**
- **Leadership Development**

Some of the most inspiring expert lecturers delivered subjects like Robotics, Astronaut Training, American Society, and Dressing for Success. The interactive workshops included exercises addressing teenage pregnancy prevention, resume writing, mock job interviews and teaching study skill techniques to classmates.

Throughout the evolution of the fraternity's involvement, fraternity members volunteered their time to tutor, mentor, deliver content and mobilize other community volunteers. These volunteers also offered the students positive African American members of the community from a variety of professions and areas of expertise. Volunteers included corporate managers, private business owners, educators, engineers, law enforcement professionals and those from many other disciplines.

One of the focus areas helped improve the students' understanding of African American contributions to American society, culture and business. Each session served to enlighten and to motivate, instilling a sense of pride in who the student is and what his or her potential is.

One of the regular guest lecturers was William Nettles, retired IBM software engineer, who brought his enormous knowledge and passion for history to the students. During his tenure, he delivered topics and people's contributions from the early settlement of the United States to contemporary events showing the relationships. Below Bill discusses his involvement with Project WORD over the four-year period.

When asked to join the Alpha project (I am a Sigma), it was a complex and compound decision with yes not the most likely response. I had to weigh two past experiences. One was running a very successful tutoring program for the Sigmas many years ago (1960's) in the Soundview section of The Bronx, New York. The other was as a professor of political economy at several New Jersey colleges in the 1970's. Overriding these experiences was a deep knowledge of American society nurtured from an early age – nine to be specific – that enabled me to write a column focused on the American Black historical experience for a local paper while in high school and later to provide a series of American Society college courses. Usually these had names such as American Society: The Alienation of the Blacks, or American Society: Migrants, Sharecroppers and Mountaineers; or American Society: The Hispanics, etc. These courses were provided against the background of the overview course – American Society: 1619 to 2010 and Beyond – that provides the integrative fabric of historical fact from Jamestown on and ensuing cultural relationships to the present similar to Tocqueville's (1835) examination of the three major races in democracy in America that make up this complex society. Then there was my perspective on tutoring programs such as this, the need for them and their effectiveness.

The need for programs such as Alpha/Project WORD is undeniable and nationwide. Unfortunately, the need is also long-standing and enduring as I can testify from my experience running a program in the Bronx in the 60's. I believe that one reason that the dismal academic achievement of Black students persists is a disconnect between home and school. This was so clear to me in the 1960's that I would not allow a student to participate in the Sigma tutoring program unless the prospective student first came with a parent to be interviewed by me personally. And that connection would last as long as the student was in the program. That Alpha/Project WORD had similar connectivity to the home was persuasive. Actual tutoring in specific courses – such as algebra – is not really the main issue. The laser-like focus on STEM courses alone does not address the broader spectrum of school relevance to life for 15 year old children. My previous experience with low-achieving students in my tutoring program and in certain college courses taught me that it was possible to provide serious academic work to such students, as long as they perceived it to be relevant, and that they would reach to grasp it. So my challenge was to craft my unique knowledge so that I could deliver a relevant body of information to the class at a college level. This last point was important. The students recognize that they are being respected as intelligent people expected to use their minds at a high level. This is a subtle point but critical since it is frequently not present in algebra or science class. This was knowledge that one could be proud to possess. The pedagogical craftsmanship involved packaging the material to make it readily accessible to this high school audience, which, though intelligent, was not well read.

I decided to say "Yes" because this was a program for Black kids. I felt that my contribution could be pivotal. The Black alienation within American society is deep and profound. By age 15 it can be almost fully formed within an individual. It corresponds in some complex way with failure in school and much more. Culturally, the roots of this alienation are denied by the larger society leaving Black individuals in a suspended duality where the real facts of our lives are denied by the larger society. Literature is replete with references to this alienation from DuBois' *"Behind the Veil,"* Richard Wright's *"Native Son"* or Ralph Ellison's *"Invisible Man"* and many more. It would be wrong not to mention in this context, James Baldwin. Listen to the political banter on the airwaves. There is a consequence from the proliferation of "stand your ground" laws (Trevon Martin; Jordan Davis) of draconian punishments that lead to ruinous incarcerations and the family stress it causes. So when I talked to the students I listened to how they used pronouns like "they" and "them" when talking about the school– unless they were on an athletic team or in the band–instead of "we" or "us". This is a special need that requires special sensitivity. My contribution to Alpha/Project Word had to address– and counteract–this alienation. A critical decision was to make extensive use of materials that the students could access easily on YouTube or the local Public Broadcasting Station. Each lecture was accompanied by a two or three page write-up by me, usually with a photo of the person who was the focus of the subject matter. This gave the students written material that they could read and discuss beyond the confines of the classroom. Each packet featured people whose significance–in one way or another—spanned years, decades and centuries as the focal point of a single lecture and as part of the larger cultural fabric. People featured included Sarjee Baartman; Thomas Jefferson & Sally Hemming; Roots: Toby's Name; A. Phillip Randolph; Fannie Lou Hammer; Tuskegee Air Men; and Dorothy Height. When certain notables died (Odetta; Miriam Mekeba; John Hope Franklin, Eartha Kitt, Lena Horne, Whitney Houston, etc.) the class paid special homage to them by describing their contributions and/or playing their music using available YouTube clips. The wide gaps such as those between Jamestown (1619) and the mid-18th century (Hat Act, etc.) were bridged by lectures that made connections between ethnic groups (White; Black; Native American) and the developing society making note that along the way, all the Black individuals dropped off at Jamestown in 1619, were free men by 1641. The reasons were complex, religiously ambiguous, and not extended to their progeny. Similarly, the gap between 1750, or so, and 1825, was bridged by examining the life of Thomas Jefferson and his relationship with Sally Hemmings. Thomas Jefferson died on July 4, 1825, with Sally Hemmings attending at his bedside.

One great leap from 1789 (Baartman - "The Hottentot Venus") was to use the life, death and eventual interment (1994) of Saartje Baartman (1789 – 29 December 1815), a South African slave woman who was taken to France and displayed nude, freak show style, for paying customers. She died within a couple of years and her preserved corpse was exhibited for many decades much to the consternation of her people. After prolonged protests and negotiation, her body was finally returned to her home in 1994 where she was put to rest with respectful fanfare. Even Nelson Mandela attended. Saartje Baartman was selected for the class because of her compelling saga that stretched for not years but centuries. But for this class more was needed to knit the pieces together. For this I chose the backstory for Amazing Grace. This song was sung in slave owners' pews as well as in the shacks of their human property. It was sung, as Tocqueville noted (1835), along the Trail of Tears, it was sung when the Berlin Wall tumbled down, and outside the courthouse of Trevon Martin's trial. It spans the great Middle Passage (Ma'afa) and was written by John Newton, a captain of a slave ship turned priest. Fortunately, I had the help of a compelling YouTube historical presentation of Amazing Grace by Whintley Phipps. He covers John Newton well. As a plus he throws in an interesting tidbit on the pentatonic (all the black keys on the piano) scale. Then he tops it off with his resounding version of Amazing Grace that brought the class to its feet for a standing O!

Alpha/Project WORD was an unqualified success. It had a lot of moving parts and provided an environment within the school campus that by its very presence created a sense of belonging that effectively countered the forces of alienation. Its wrap-around services including mentorship, calls and visits to the home, pizza on tutoring days and placement in special schools to facilitate graduation were all essential to the program. My other contribution was to use my extensive background as a retired engineer to tutor in math and science courses.

How did I do?

There are two phases of my contributions based on the foundation course (American Society: 1619-2010 and Beyond). The first was directed at the all-Black audience. The core of the course is the development of American Society of which black people are a critical part. There was rapt attention to and identification with the compelling life and times of Saartje Baartman -- the Hottentot Venus. The YouTube clip from "Roots" where Kunte Kinte is whipped in order to force him to accept his new name (Toby) was brutal to watch. There were actual tears. Someone in the class complained that it was too brutal. They will not forget it!

We spent considerable time on Thomas Jefferson and Sally Hemmings. Why? Primarily because when Jefferson sent for Sally to join him in France where he served as ambassador, Sally was 14 years old – the same age as the girls in the class. They could – and did – identify with Sally. Why did she return to Monticello? Her older brother James made sure she knew that when she arrived in France, she was free. She did not have to return three years later at age 17 – pregnant! It was a compelling life that – especially for the girls – made an indelible impression on these young people, one they will never forget. They may not remember the Louisiana Purchase (1804) and they may forget Lewis and Clark, but they cannot forget the young Native American woman who led them into the wilderness.

Another example was "the old lady." One day when I entered the room where Alpha/Project WORD was housed, a couple of the students were scurrying around and chattering about "the old lady." They were searching the textbooks for information on Dorothy Height. She had been a subject in about three of my lectures and a couple of YouTube clips that I played since I knew she was at the end of her life. They were tremendously impressed by Dr. Height and knew she was quite ill. They saw her in a YouTube clip seated left of Dr. Martin Luther King, Jr. as he delivered his "I Have a Dream" speech and they wanted to know more about her. They asked out loud, "How come the things that Mr. Nettles tells us is not in our textbooks?" Indeed!

These examples and others like Fanny Lou Hammer; A. Phillip Randolph; Bayard Rustin; Stokely Carmichael; Chick Webb, Lena Horne and Emmitt Till provide a rich framework against which to array some of their life experiences where, had they not had this experience there otherwise could have been a void.

The Opportunity Class welcomed all comers with a large percentage of black students. This did not change the course since it is based on American Society: 1619-

2010 and Beyond. The difference between the Alpha/Project WORD class and the Opportunity class is in the choice of elements to be emphasized.

For instance, the Jamestown experience involves more in depth discussion of farm record books and relationships between the three (white, Native American, and black) races so that the analysis aligns more directly with Tocqueville's Democracy in America (1831). Time is allocated to Hispanics also due to the prominent place this group plays in current, especially political, discourse. So the subject matter is the same but shuffled a bit to map the movement of the frontier from east to west to borrow a metaphor from Thorsten Veblen. Not to use Veblen's model directly but because it provides a background against which one can discuss the "Trail of Tears"; Texas and the Alamo; Red states/Blue states; Slavery North/South; etc. And since, in the Opportunity Class classroom, there was a large map of the United States on the wall.

Much of the material like the Whintley Phipps "Amazing Grace" YouTube clip received a standing ovation just like in the Alpha/Project WORD class. But with the emphasis shifted from the black experience to a broader perspective, it was necessary to focus on themes that resonate in a multi-ethnic class like Red State/Blue State (The ancestors of the heroes of the Alamo vote Republican!). As the frontier moved west, the nation consumed Louisiana, Texas, and finally California. The

Peculiar Institution of Slavery divided the country and a civil war cost over 600,000 lives. The lasting aftershocks of these events reverberate to this day and will for some time to come. However, the impact of this material is different in a mixed class. This should not be a surprise. Sally Hemmings age 14, can be very impactful for a black girl age 14 or 15 where it may not be as compelling for a white girl of 14 or 15. The "old lady" – Dorothy Height – was an amazing person that had an important impact in the Alpha/Project WORD. This intergroup ability to identify with the material is what is sacrificed when the broader Opportunity Class to as much African American history. Both classes, however, were very successful. One – Alpha/Project WORD — was just far more impactful than the other. The pedagogical techniques used in both courses were the same: YouTube clips; brief class notes; compelling and engaging presentation. In one case – Alpha/Project WORD – there was the overt intention to use information in order to impact alienation within the group. It is important to understand that there is a very real, and serious problem with education for black students in this country. Alpha/Project WORD was very successful. It is important to understand why the program worked and what part my classes played in that success. First, it had wrap around services together with a strong tutoring component and good relations with teachers.

As I write this it just so happens to be May 17th exactly sixty years after the 1954 Brown vs. Board of

Education Supreme Court 9/0 decision that placed a capstone on the segregation epoch of America. Today Thurgood Marshall hardly warrants half a page in the high school textbook. Segregation has returned to 1954 level and in some jurisdictions – mainly in the north – it is even greater.

"Brown" did not end segregation, it outlawed it. Nor did it do anything to improve education! It disrupted American society and unleashed a backlash that continues today. However, much of the argument and supportive data leading to the decision emphasized psychological damage of segregated schools. Works such as Gunnar Myrdal's *American Dilemma: The Negro Problem and Modern Democracy* (1944) and Kenneth B. Clark's famous doll studies that have been repeated many times and that vividly underscores psychological damage – by preference for white dolls and rejection of black dolls – by black children at very early ages.

The "dilemma" Myrdal described is a situation wherein "whites oppressed negroes and then pointed to negroes poor performance as reason for the oppression." Today these observations reverberate through American Society – not Ryan's budget - ways that affect each person to one degree or another. It has a profound impact on the young as they are formed and shaped by institutions and culture that surrounds and molds them – family; media; school; law enforcement; etc. By ninth grade, although the impact may vary from individual to individual, the effect has been well documented by an unbroken string of writers from DuBois, Richard Wright, Ralph Ellison, James Baldwin – to name a few. Ellison wrote in a review of Myrdal's *Dilemma* in 1944 that "…it is not unusual for a Negro to experience a sensation that he does not exist in the real world at all. He seems rather, to exist in the…fantasy of the white American mind…"

In 1947 Ellison embedded the metaphor of the *Invisible Man* in his major work where I encountered it in 1951. As a description it fit many of the black friends, relatives, schoolmates, neighbors and acquaintances pursuing the American dream from – as DuBois put it – "behind the veil". The dark side of this "invisibility" is alienation as a consequence of oppressive cultural elements that intrude – even dominate – many lives in the black community: A profound alienation and disconnection from American Society that cannot be ignored in our schools.

Outside of the school-based activities, Alpha also offered other services like the Rites of Passage program. Oak Grove had the opportunity to participate in this program, which promised "Boys Will Come and Men Will Return". Each student, regardless of academic performance, entered the program and returned as a much more focused student who was equipped to provide leadership in a variety of areas. One student started the Fall session with all F's. After the first semester, the student's grades went from all classes failed to A's and B's in all classes proving that attitude can allow aptitude to show through and be realized. So, why does it take an attitude-changing program like the Rites of Passage to mobilize a black boy to achieve his true potential? Another student was very withdrawn and introverted but started to blossom after completing the Rites of Passage, ultimately graduating on time and being recognized for his artist talents.

College members of the fraternity also reaped added benefits when they were able to get paid for tutoring by joining with Project WORD's partner, Xcel Tutoring Services. It was very clear that the high school students responded very positively with college students who were closer to their age and life experiences. Although, the college students did not have teaching experience, their knowledge of the subject matter and student techniques made their contribution valuable to the program.

The mentoring component of the program resulted in many life-changing experiences. Often, these mentoring opportunities arose during discipline moments. Teachers gained confidence in the program and the ability of the volunteers to motivate proper behavior. In one case, a teacher noted that a student had disrespected her in the classroom. The student was told in no uncertain terms that that behavior was unacceptable in spite of protest that the teacher showed disrespect first. This student was returned to the teacher's classroom for an apology. Although protesting the entire trip across campus, the student made a gracious apology to the teacher in front of the entire class. Creating an effective learning environment requires mutual respect amongst all stakeholders.

There were several other programs supported during this experience. The Opportunity Class designed to help rising sophomores recover credit for failing Mathematics and English during their freshman year. Recognizing the success of the class and realizing that black students were not selected; Project WORD funded the class with the requirement that fifty percent of the students be African American. Members of the fraternity's team volunteered to assist in the delivery of that year's program. Being involved in this class gave volunteers more opportunities to meet students in need and win their confidence.

Some of the lectures and workshops were deemed valuable enough to warrant a special assembly inviting a broader student population. One exciting session featured a robot designer who had also trained to be a NASA astronaut. His lecture was so interesting that several science teachers brought their classes. Ujima Family Services, another on campus service provider, also brought their students to the session. The lecturer was able to captivate the audience with his experiences designing robots for military, personal, medical and instructional purposes. His experience in astronaut training gave students insight into new career consideration while hearing it from a person with a similar background.

Another exciting workshop featured a video entitled, "Bring Your A Game" by Mario Van Peeples. It was used to focus on preventing dropouts.

Former NASA Engineer Harold Clay organized a field trip and provided regular mentorship to several students.

Throughout the years of engagement, changes in the school's culture can be attributed to the programming, mentoring and tutoring provided. When the school became a Program Improvement School, its recovery plan included this program as one of its action items. School staff used the program as a resource for students in need. Parents directed their students to the program and worked closely with team to help their student achieve their academic goal. African American students became more visible. Each volunteer had memorable experiences.

As we look back over the years and anticipate the future, several key observations were made:

The program of volunteer involvement using the "Go to High School Go to College" curriculum coupled with Project WORD worked and made a difference for the students and the school as a whole. Students who were not on track did graduate.

The impact of positive black role models had a lasting impact on the everyday life on campus providing a sense of pride and understanding. Engaging students in high school is late but still effective. Early intervention is needed to improve study skills and habits that lead to improvement.

Chapter 7

Building Institutions

One of my closest confidantes during the time of my difficult divorce was Gail Ortega. Articulate, well-read, passionate, committed to the uplift of African people, Gail was a Black man who everyone assumed was a Latina because of his name! Gail's name was a result of having a father with Cuban roots. While he lived in the Bay Area for decades, Gail was the most sought-after Black person called upon to do libations for a myriad of community gatherings. Once during one of our long conversations about how to best advance our people, Gail pointed out that I had helped start three institutions that were all thriving—the Santa Clara County Alliance of Black Educators (SCCABE), the California Alliance of African American Educators (CAAAE) and the Dr. Frank S. Greene Scholars Program (GSP). I had never thought of myself as a builder of institutions, but since that day I do realize that I am.

I mentioned in an earlier chapter that I helped start the SCCABE with other people like Brenda Smith and

Sandra Mack. From 1994 to 2001, I served as the president. During my tenure, I helped strengthen its infrastructure and was able to pass it on to Leon Beauchman who has been president since then. What makes the SCCABE's longevity so remarkable is that it has never had a robust budget, does not have a 501(c)3 and relies on all volunteers to carry out its mission. Incredibly committed people like Annie Handy, Carolyn Johnson, Josephine Miles, Antoinette Battiste, Deborah Raymond, Cyd Matthias and Barbara Boone have stayed involved and unselfishly devote countless hours year after year. For about 30 years, the SCCABE has been focused on doing whatever is necessary to help improve the educational outcomes for Black students throughout Silicon Valley.

The signature event of the SCCABE is its annual Cultural Pursuits Awards Ceremony. Held each spring to celebrate graduating 5th/6th, 8th and 12th graders in categories ranging from Improved Grade Point Average to Civic Involvement and Spiritual Consciousness, this event celebrated its 25th year in May 2014. Thousands of students have been honored during this time and many have gone on to have illustrious careers. Lynford Goddard is one of those students. He was the first Black valedictorian at Santa Clara High School in 1994. He went to Stanford University on a full scholarship and earned a BS degree in physics with a minor in Japanese. I had the privilege of attending Lynford's undergraduate graduation and sat next to his physics adviser. That professor told me that Lynford was the best physics student he had ever taught. Just months earlier, that professor had earned a Nobel Prize in physics! Lynford went on to earn a PhD in physics at Stanford and immediately landed a job as an assistant professor at the University of Illinois at Urbana. Recognized by President Barack Obama in a White House setting honoring the top 100 promising scientists under 40 years old, Lynford soon gained tenure at the university and continues to spearhead remarkable research while giving back to his community and inspiring other under-represented students to pursue careers in STEM (science, technology, engineering, math). Lynford's is just one of countless stories like this of Black students we honored going on to become productive members of American society.

If I am in town, I do not miss the Cultural Pursuits Ceremony because it is so inspiring. Many parents have shared with me that recognizing their students in elementary school on a stage with hundreds of family members, friends and community members beaming with pride in the audience helped keep the children encouraged to do their best all the way through middle and high school. Some parents have told me over the years that it was at this ceremony that their children got their first recognition ever from school. The program was so successful that it has been replicated in the Oak Grove School District under the visionary leadership of its former superintendent Manny Barbara. That district actually starts its awards at the third grade level. Just imagine what kind of impact that can have!

Students are nominated by school administrators, teachers, counselors, or community members. Each nominee must have a grade point average of 2.5 or better except in the category of Improved GPA and Academics – Grade Point Average. For Black and Brown communities seeking to do something to affirm its children, the Cultural Pursuits Awards Ceremony is easy to replicate. A stellar example of this is what happened when the CAAAE's chapter, the Southern Alameda County Alliance of African American Educators (SACAAAE), decided to do just that. Under the outstanding leadership of Bobbie Brooks, at the time Assistant Superintendent in the Alameda County Office of Education (ACOE), who was the founder of SACAAAE, the model was taken to another level of excellence. In its first year, there were only 24 students honored and about 100 people were at the ceremony held in the boardroom of the ACOE. By its second year, over 100 students were honored and the event was held in the theater at Cal State East Bay with a standing-room only crowd of 500 people. By its third year, the event had to be moved to Cal State East Bay's gymnasium because several hundred students were honored and nearly 1,000 people showed up to celebrate them. In its fourth year, SACAAAE partnered with Chabot College in Hayward,

CA to accommodate the hundreds of students it was now honoring and the hordes of people who nearly filled the theater that seats 1,432. For the next five years, SACAAAE held its ceremony at Chabot. In 2013, Bobbie merged SACAAAE with the Southern Alameda County Regional Educational Alliance (SACREA) to form the African American Regional Educational Alliance (AAREA). This new organization not only, never skipped a beat when it took over the student awards ceremony, but it has added dimensions that make it a new model. Although SACAAAE did have a 501(c)3, it never had a robust budget or a paid staff, but its committed volunteers (like Robyn Fisher, Ric Ricard, Mary Fisher, Wanda Williams, and Andrea Wilson) exemplified servant leadership and many children and their families have been positively impacted in powerful ways that only personal histories will ever reveal.

What if instead of wringing our hands about what to do to help Black and Brown students succeed in schools that were never designed for them, their own communities decided to host Cultural Pursuits ceremonies annually? While I realize that this is a very tiny thing to do, it is better than nothing. There are too many communities throughout this country that never come together to celebrate its children. We can change that. Are you in?!

In the appendix, I have included the forms used to solicit nominations as well as a page from a sample program. Visit You Tube to see a short video of the SCCABE's 2014 awards ceremony and be uplifted!

In addition to its annual awards ceremony, the SCCABE also hosts a Back-to-School Social so that educators in the region can network, encourage each other, hear guest speakers and welcome new Black educators. Each year for about the last five, the SCCABE has partnered with Tabia (a local theatrical group) to expose Black high school students to Black plays and lead them in dynamic discussions about the pieces. Over the years, the SCCABE has sponsored Parent Empowerment conferences, promoted a college-going culture and videotaped students, educators and community leaders bearing witness to conditions in area schools that impair and promote student achievement.

Another institution that I founded in 2001 after I left the presidency of the SCCABE is the CAAAE. In chapter 4, I discussed some of the work of the CAAAE, but here is where I will write about the people who were members of my founding board, some of our early accomplishments on a shoestring budget, the great work the CAAAE has seeded all over this country, and what we are incubating now that will affect millions of Black and Brown children nationwide.

After attending conferences of the National Alliance of Black School Educators (NABSE) for 20 consecutive years, I had become friends with many affiliate presidents from around the state of CA. In order to become a statewide affiliate, I had to garner the support of the active affiliates in CA. I consulted with James Taylor who was the president at the time of the San Francisco Alliance of Black School Educators (SFABSE) and Ellen Posey who was president of the Oakland Alliance of Black Educators (OABE). For about one year in 1998, we would meet at the Hyatt Hotel in Burlingame (almost midway between Oakland, San Francisco and San Jose) to discuss what the CAAAE would look like. Tragically, Ellen contracted cancer and died. We were all devastated and stopped meeting for an entire year while we grieved such a large loss. Since we realized that Ellen would have wanted us to continue the work, we re-grouped and started meeting again. By then, Clifford Thompson was president of OABE and in his hallmark affable and always positive manner jumped right in to help us with the plans. Lynne Murray, a fellow teacher in the ESUHSD, was an officer in the SCCABE and we were joined at the hip during this time period. We spent hours on the road to Burlingame and at the Hyatt discussing what would become the CAAAE.

Once we had the foundation established, I knew that there was a key person who I needed to accept the role of treasurer. I had known William (Bill) Ellerbee since I had joined the SDA Church in 1977. We worked together on the board of the Greater Bay Area (GBA) Youth Association—an organization that brought young, Black Seventh-day Adventists together quarterly for events like

Bible quiz bowls, socials, empowerment workshops, etc. Bill was also treasurer at Capital City SDA Church in Sacramento and a gifted pianist there. Ironically, he was close friends with my ex-husband's oldest brother. Bill had an impeccable reputation in and outside of the SDA church and his integrity was often lauded. Bill was an administrator in the Sacramento Unified School District at that time. After Bill agreed to be treasurer, I knew that the CAAAE would become a great organization.

I then had to reach out to affiliate presidents throughout the state to ask if they would be willing to serve in some capacity as board members of the CAAAE. The first president I asked was James Taylor of the SFABSE. James was a pillar in his community. Well-known for his stellar principal-ship of the Dr. Martin Luther King, Jr. Academic Middle School, I asked James to be Vice President and he agreed. In our plans, we decided that there should be what we called then membership coordinators in each region who lived in that region and could help us grow it. Cliff Thompson agreed to be the coordinator for the Bay Area Region. The outstanding president and founder of the Valley Alliance of African American School Educators (VAAASE), Dr. Rosaline Bessard, warmly accepted my invitation to be the coordinator of what we called the Valley Region (Fresno/Bakersfield/Central Valley) and became one of the CAAAE's most enthusiastic promoters. At Bill Ellerbee's recommendation, I reached out to his colleagues in the Sacramento area who were active in the Elk Grove Alliance of Black School Educators (EGABSE)—Barbara Evans and Princetta Purkins. At the time, Barbara was Executive Director of EGABSE and Princetta was president. Barbara agreed to be the coordinator for the Sacramento/Stockton region and Princetta became the CAAAE's secretary. They were both great additions to our growing board of directors. Since NABSE did not have an affiliate in San Diego, we had to ask people who lived in the city for someone who could represent that area. Lynwood Taylor's name came up early in our search and when I asked him to join the CAAAE, he enthusiastically accepted and was a real asset during his tenure.

Because of some internecine politics that I will not share here, the Los Angeles Alliance of Black School Educators (LABSE) did not choose to join our budding organization so I had to look elsewhere for a coordinator for that region. At the time, I was on a state-wide committee for National Board Certification and attended a meeting in Sacramento where I struck up a conversation about the CAAAE with the amazing Anne Ifekwunigwe. At the time, she was an elementary school teacher in the Los Angeles Unified School District (LAUSD) and was running a center in partnership with the University of California at Los Angeles (UCLA) to increase the number of Black teachers who would become National Board-certified. I recognized Anne's brilliance during our short time together at the NBCT meeting and asked her on the spot if she would be interested in becoming the CAAAE's coordinator for the Los Angeles region. I cannot recall if she accepted right away or after we had several phone conversations and email exchanges, but soon Anne was an enthusiastic member of our board. The youngest member of our board, Anne's youthful vigor, intellectual acumen and passion for people of African ancestry contributed a great deal to those early years of the CAAAE. While all of the other board members left after about 3-5 years (except James Taylor who still serves) due to changes in personal circumstances or retirement, Anne left to enroll at Harvard in a doctoral program and went on to earn a PhD in urban leadership and is now a superintendent. She continues to positively affect the lives of many children.

The accomplishments of this remarkably talented founding board and those who took their places (see complete list in the introduction) could fill up a separate book, but I will focus on two that I think readers can benefit most from learning about—our decade of stellar summer institutes and our STEM program.

The CAAAE was officially launched in October 2001 with a reception and plated dinner for 250 people at the Renaissance Parc Hotel in San Francisco. Completely funded by the corporate sponsor who had consistently underwritten the annual Cultural Pursuits Awards Ceremony of the SCCABE described earlier in this chapter, Houghton Mifflin's support of this elegant launch was spearheaded by Paul Griffin. At the time, Paul was the Director of Urban Affairs for the Western Region of Houghton Mifflin and loved supporting our work. He is currently a Vice President for the company and a founding board member of A Black Education Network (ABEN)—the next generation of my work detailed in chapter 9. I would be remiss to not mention the amazing support also given to the launch by Melissa Williams and Charlie Cordova. That night, 150 people joined the CAAAE and each new member was given a leather-bound portfolio with the CAAAE's and Houghton Mifflin's names on it and three books relevant to people of African ancestry professionally packaged and tied with a ribbon.

From the inception of the CAAAE, I knew that professional development needed to be central to the services provided to people who work with Black students. Because I had earned my master's degree in education and lifetime teaching credentials in English, French and psychology from Stanford University's School of Education, I picked up the phone one day and called Professor Linda Darling Hammond who I had recently read about in their newsletter when she was appointed. From the very beginning, Linda was warm, friendly and excited about partnering with the brand new CAAAE to host two-day summer institutes. Linda insisted that they could not be "sit-and-get" sessions, but rather engaging and practical. She asked her colleague at the time, Charla Rolland, to work with me on the design of the institute. Charla and I spent countless hours getting it just right. We decided that we would have a nationally-renowned keynoter to kick off the first morning, then we would have two speakers that afternoon. On Day 2, people would "go deeper" with one of the three speakers from the first day. Their charge after lunch would be to go anywhere on the campus and work with someone or alone on a professional development plan that they could implement in their sphere of influence. They would be asked to present that plan to all attendees in the last two hours of Day 2. In July 2002, we held our first two-day institute at Stanford. Since race was central to the conversation and we wanted people to feel comfortable discussing it, we limited attendance to 60 people. Thanks to a relationship that James Taylor had with the brilliant Dr. Bob Moses of the Algebra Project, we were able to secure that civil rights veteran and MacArthur genius award-winner to keynote that first institute. The response to the institute was overwhelming! We finally had to cut off attendance at 94 people due to space limitations and we turned away at least 100 people. We realized that we had struck a chord with educators in California. They did not know how to successfully reach African American students and they were eager to learn how.

For the next nine years, our keynoters read like a Who's Who in Black education. In 2003, I secured Dr.

Beverly Daniel Tatum (author of *Why Are All the Black Kids Sitting Together in the Cafeteria and Other Conversations about Race*), newly-selected president of my daughter's undergraduate alma mater (Spelman College), by offering to host a Northern California gathering of Spelman alums and their guests the night of her keynote. Thanks to my friend and colleague, Lakiba Pittman, we were able to host a very nice event at Agilent Technologies just down the street from Stanford's campus. About 100 Spelman alumnae and supporters from all over the Bay Area attended the event were Dr. Tatum discussed her vision for the leading college for Black women in the United States. Our keynoter in 2004 was Dr. Gloria Ladson-Billings. She has written a number of best-selling books, but is best known for the seminal *Dreamkeepers: Successful Teachers of Black Students*. One of the most prolific, incisive and witty women I know, Dr. Ladson-Billings is the consummate teacher's teacher. In much demand to keynote, she speaks all over the world. At our third institute in 2005, we featured Dr. Pedro Noguera. He has written so many books that it's best to just Google him!

I wanted our fifth annual institute in 2006 to be especially powerful so I invited three Black intellectual rock stars: Dr. Wade Nobles was our keynote speaker. One of the brilliant founders of the Association of Black Psychologists (ABPsi), Dr. Nobles had earned his PhD at Stanford years earlier, but because of the "radical" nature of his writing and ardent advocacy for African people, he had never been invited back to speak. That year we met in Kresge Auditorium in the law school and attracted our largest number of attendees to date—154 people, and we still had to turn away some! The other two giants that year were Dr. Joyce King (the Benjamin E. Mays Endowed Chair for Urban Teaching, Learning and Leadership at Georgia State University, and immediate past president of the American Educational Research Association) and Dr. Noma LeMoine (former director of the highly-successful Academic English Mastery Program in Los Angeles Unified School District). The audience was riveted by all three presentations and the institute garnered, as usual, exceptional evaluations. While I felt it would be difficult to follow the fifth institute with one as powerful, I was mistaken! In 2007, we featured one of my personal favorite writers, Dr. Lisa Delpit, world-renowned for the best-selling book entitled *Other People's Children*. Lisa scored a homerun and had the audience begging for more. By the time of our seventh institute, I wanted attendees to see some of the pedagogy and practices of the previous six years in action at a school site so I invited Dr. Sharroky Hollie to keynote in 2008. Dr. Hollie was one of the founders of the Culture and Language Academy of Success (CLAS) in the Los Angeles area. When I visited his school, I was almost brought to tears because there I saw Black students who were joyful learners, well-behaved and proud of their

African ancestry. When Sharroky shared his work through word and actual videos, the audience was in awe. Several school districts actually employed Sharroky and he continues to positively influence the field through his consulting company. Because the CAAAE is a statewide organization and we had held all of our previous institutes at Stanford and because one of our co-coordinators for the Los Angeles region at the time (Marsha Horsley) had a close relationship with Center X at UCLA, I decided to move the institute to that campus in 2009. We brought back Dr. Bob Moses because California was still wringing its hands about how to teach Algebra to Black and Brown students and through his Algebra Project, Dr. Moses had done that successfully with hundreds of the most poverty-stricken students in the nation. I also invited then Superintendent of Public Instruction for the state of California, Jack O'Connell, to address the attendees because I was serving on a statewide P-16 committee tasked with recommending policies to close what the CAAAE calls the "opportunity" gap. In addition to Dr. Moses, we had excellent presenters in Dr. Gail Thompson and Dr. Tyrone Howard, yet our attendance was the lowest we had ever experienced since after the first institute. Because it was our first time at UCLA and the staff I worked with in Center X (Dr. Jody Priselac and her wonderful Administrative Assistant whose name escapes me) was so great, I decided to try it again on that campus the next year (2010). I felt that California was now ready to learn about African-centered education so I asked Dr. King to recommend someone who was highly-regarded in that field. Since Dr. Carol Lee was the first person that she mentioned, that is whom I sought out. Dr. Lee warmly accepted my invitation to keynote our 9th annual institute. Although she was a phenomenal speaker, attendance was still disappointingly lower than our expectations.

I decided to return to Stanford for what would become our tenth and final institute in 2011. I convinced the CAAAE board of directors that it was time to cease sponsoring them because I had discovered that people were not getting traction with the pedagogies and practices once they returned to the field primarily due to institutional racism. I felt that the next decade of the CAAAE's work should focus on making the ground fertile for the new knowledge that our attendees were gaining from the best and the brightest Black educators from throughout the country by focusing on policy. To end with a bang, I changed the entire structure of the institute. For the first time, I invited non-Black presenters. One of them was the remarkable Manny Barbara—a highly-decorated former superintendent of the Oak Grove School District in San Jose, California. I had worked with Manny for about 20 years at that point and he had become my model of an anti-racist White leader who not only understood the effects of institutional racism, but had run a school district for years bent on dismantling those practices. I wanted Manny to show how he had gone about doing that. During his presentation, he involved another equity warrior from Oak Grove—Assistant Superintendent Barbara Service. I had worked closely with Barbara when I coordinated the work of Partners in School Innovation years earlier and had been impressed with her passion for justice. From the first time I had started coordinating the institutes, I had always wanted Dr. Geneva Gay to be one of the keynoters. I had spoken to her about it several times, but she was never available for various reasons. Since this was going to be our final one, I called and compelled her to attend! Not only did she agree, she cancelled one of her university classes so that she could make the trip from the state of Washington to California. I was thrilled and she did not disappoint. The author of *Culturally Relevant Pedagogy*, Dr. Gay's book is considered the "bible" for students learning about this practice and is widely used in schools of education around the world. Because of my close affiliation with Dr. Joyce King, I had attended several national conferences of the American Educational Research Association (AERA). One of the methods used to give feedback on presentations is to have respondents. I decided to do that for our institute so I asked Dr. King to serve as well as Dr. John Browne (author of one of my favorite books for transforming schools entitled *Walking the Equity Talk: A Guide to Transforming School Communities*) and Dr. Ken Magdaleno (a highly-respected professor at Fresno State University in California who is my model for Latino educational activism). Ironically, I had introduced Dr. Browne to Dr. Magdaleno a few years earlier. John subsequently profiled Ken as an example of a culturally courageous leader in *Walking the Equity Talk*. Not only was that final institute well-attended, I considered it the best of the ten.

With the institute's chapter closed, the CAAAE is now focused on policy. I serve on several statewide committees related to teacher credentialing, school discipline and climate, and the Local Control Funding Formula (LCFF). The latter is California's first major reform in about 40 years relative to how public schools are funded. The CAAAE's coordinators around the state are paying very close attention to how the Local Control Accountability Plans (LCAP) mandated by LCFF are being implemented in districts in their regions to ascertain whether they will have an impact on the academic achievement and social-emotional well-being of Black students.

To round out this chapter, I will share a little about the third institution that I founded that is still thriving. Because I will be writing my next book exclusively about it, I will give a broad overview here. Established in 2001 when the CAAAE was also launched, I named our STEM (science, technology, engineering, math) program after an African American scientist who helped pave the way for today's computers and made his fortune in Silicon

Valley along the way. When our daughter was a teenager, she had babysat for Dr. Frank S. Greene's daughter and son-in-law (Angela and Henry Gage). Henry's father (Henry Gage, Sr.) was my first real role model. He was one of the first Black people to serve on the board of trustees of the East Side Union High School District (ESUHSD) in San Jose, California, and had pressed the administration about hiring more Black teachers. I was one of those hired in 1977 while Mr. Gage was still on the board. We developed a lifelong love and respect for each other and he frequently boasted with pride about my accomplishments. He passed away in 2014 and is greatly missed by many whose lives he positively impacted.

The GSP is modeled after an earlier program that I helped start with two Black men from a now defunct non-profit called the Healing Institute. In 1998, Halim Mustafa and Rasheed Salaam spent hours working with me at my kitchen table to create the Dr. George Washington Carver Scholars Program (CSP). Halim and Rasheed had been traveling around the country trying to get cities to hold science fairs to commemorate a national holiday on the Congressional calendar (Public Law 290) observing Dr. Carver's date of death—January 5. His date of birth was unknown. While I was still president of the Santa Clara County Alliance of Black Educators (SCCABE), they approached us about joining them in that effort. At its height, the CSP had 254 Black students from throughout Silicon Valley and our funders were extensive. For three consecutive years beginning on January 5, 1999, we held science fairs so large that we had to use the Santa Clara Convention Center. Our awards galas were also smashing successes and topped nearly 1,200 attendees in the third and final year of the CSP's existence. Due to differences in how to grow the CSP, I left as chief coordinator and it died within a few months. It was a very traumatic time for me and an extremely hard decision, but it had to be made.

Some parents who had been in the CSP literally begged me to start a similar STEM program and that is how the GSP came to exist. From its onset, we borrowed some of the best practices from the CSP. One involved training parents on how to help us run the GSP. To this day, parents are still the backbone of the GSP even though I hired the amazing Gloria Whitaker-Daniels as the director after its first seven years under my leadership and she now has two outstanding program managers, Kim Bomar and Gina Hendy, and an administrative assistant, Karen Gage (the wife of another son of Henry Gage's). Gloria is a super bright mechanical engineer by training whose three children all went through the GSP while I was the leader. Krystina, her oldest, earned a B.S. degree in neuroscience from Pomona College. Her second child, Kathryn, has BS and MS degrees in biomedical engineering from the University of Southern California (USC) and her last child, Kolin, is studying nutritional science at San Jose State University. Gloria's husband,

Theron, is also a mechanical engineer so I call them the consummate STEM family.

The GSP meets once each month on a Saturday during the school year. The Scholars are exposed to hands-on science, supplemental math experiences, and engineering contests like building balsawood bridges and mousetrap cars. Technology is woven throughout the curriculum. Each January, the GSP holds its science fair. As of the publication of this book, there are 126 students in the GSP ranging from third grade all the way through twelfth. We stay with the students from the time they are accepted into the GSP until they graduate from high school. We do not accept students younger than third grade and older than eighth. Each summer, the GSP partners with local companies or universities to offer week-long science institutes designed to give the Scholars more intensive STEM experiences in rich environments. In 2014, we partnered with NASA for the elementary-age Scholars and they focused on Things That Fly; middle-schoolers met at Texas Instruments and learned coding; and the high school students met at Santa Clara University and had to design how music will be accessed in 20 years.

My favorite story about the GSP involves the incredibly brilliant founder of Cypress Semiconductor—Dr. T.J. Rodgers. While he was in a doctoral program studying electrical engineering at Stanford University, he created a semi-conductor and a few years after graduation launched Cypress. I met T.J. at an educational forum at a local Marriott Hotel in Silicon Valley in 1998. He was on a panel with others focused on "diversifying the pipeline" of people entering companies like Cypress by preparing them at a young age to love STEM. In addition to the Superintendent of Schools for the Santa Clara County Office of Education, the dean of the School of Engineering at the University of California at Davis was on the panel. When he complained that if Dr. Rodgers did not hire so many engineers from outside of the country, his graduates could get jobs, T.J. quickly rejoined by stating, "If your School was not 18th in the nation, perhaps I would hire your graduates! I hire the best and the brightest. I am a businessman." In the packed room of about 500 people, the silence was deafening. I cannot recall how it was broken, but we were all visibly glad when it was!

The CSP had just garnered its first $50,000 grant from Intel and I decided to stand up during the Questions & Answers period to make that public and invite others who were serious about "diversifying the pipeline" to meet me in the back of the room after the breakfast ended. The first person to approach me was a Vice President at Intel. She threw her arms around me and thanked me for making that announcement! I had no idea that she was even in the room. After her, about five other companies approached me and they formed the foundation of our first corporate donors. After my line was finished, I got in

T.J.'s. I liked his candor and told him so when it was my turn to speak with him. I also asked him if he would be interested in investing in the CSP. He said that I was the one who announced that Intel had just given the CSP its first $50,000. Right? I said, "Yes." He said, "Cypress is only half as large as Intel so I will give you $25,000. Call my office tomorrow." I tried not to appear too shaken by this unexpected gift, but when I got to my car I called Rasheed immediately and could hardly contain my excitement!

For the rest of the CSP's short life, Dr. Rodgers and Cypress were incredibly generous with their time and resources. When I told T.J. that I had left the CSP and it had died and I started the GSP and why, he seemed a little disappointed that I had abandoned Dr. Carver's name because he had personally come to admire his genius, but he still came along and has been one of the bulwarks behind the GSP's success since our inception. In 2006, the CAAAE's then board chairman, Henry Taylor (an immensely talented fundraising professional) and I paid our annual visit to Dr. Rodgers and was there to ask if we could use one of his wineries (he is a wine connoisseur) to hold the CAAAE's annual board retreat. Before we could get to that ask, we shared a PowerPoint outlining our vision for the CAAAE and GSP. The first item on the list was a need for a computer lab where the Greene Scholars could meet each Saturday and where the CAAAE offices and future employees would be located.

Dr. Rodgers stopped us there and asked how much space we needed. I was not expecting that question, but you must always be prepared so I said, "Enough for 30 computers, desks, chairs and a laser printer." He casually replied, "I can do that. Next." My board chair and I hastily exchanged startled looks, yet kept going down the list. We waited until we were in the parking lot to high-five each other! That was in June. The next day I got a call from T.J.'s administrative assistant asking if we wanted laptops or desktops. I chose laptops. By the board retreat (which was held at Cypress that August because T.J.'s main winery was still under construction), we had a ribbon-cutting with T.J., the Scholars, most of their parents and about 100 community members. About four years later, T.J.'s chief of facilities (Tom Surrette) told me that Cypress was downsizing and needed our computer lab and office space. When he had shared that with T.J., Tom said he was told that he could have the lab only if he gave the CAAAE better than what we currently had. We now have access to the entire Cypress headquarters in Silicon Valley. That is where the Scholars meet each month, the CAAAE offices are, the science fair and career fair are held and any other meetings that we have to conduct. When it comes to a CAAAE ally who happens to be White, no one matches Dr. T.J. Rodgers. No one! There is so much more to share about the GSP, but you will have to wait for my next book!

Chapter 8

A Black Education Network (ABEN)

The next chapter in my life was shaped largely by the enormous influence of one Black woman. When I was seeking a dynamic educator who would complement the huge intellect of Dr. Wade Nobles chosen to keynote the CAAAE's fifth annual institute at Stanford University, I turned to him for a recommendation. Without hesitation, he suggested Dr. Joyce King. He told me that she was an outstanding scholar who had earned her undergraduate degree with honors from Stanford and her PhD. More importantly (as far as I was concerned), she was unapologetically focused on the uplift of African people just like me. Ironically, I had known Joyce years earlier when she was coordinating the Teacher Education program at Santa Clara University and I invited her to serve on a panel to judge model schools designed by students at an alternative school (Pegasus High) where I was the charter English teacher.

After Dr. King's warm acceptance of my invitation, we became close colleagues. I marveled at her brilliance and asked her to join the CAAAE's Advisory Board/Think Tank. She graciously accepted. The more she saw of the CAAAE's work, the more she pressed me to take the model nationally. I would joke with her and say, "I cannot fight negroes locally. I certainly don't want to fight them on a national level!" Dr. King's influence soon won me over. She started by introducing me to the online community of the National Black Education Agenda (NBEA). The brainchild of Dr. Sam Anderson, I soon became a regular consumer of the powerful knowledge that he shared weekly about the plight of Black students from throughout the United States. Here I had been concerned with the fact that only about 80% of the Black students in California graduated from high school when in places like Detroit, Brooklyn, and Chicago it was often 50% or lower. I was appalled to learn that such a small percentage of our Black students were reading or doing math at grade level nationally. I felt like Jonah. God was clearly calling me to do work that could positively impact millions of our children instead of just the few thousands that the CAAAE was touching annually. At around this same time, I realized that the CAAAE was uniquely positioned to spearhead this work because we had just received our first $100,000 grant from the Kellogg Foundation.

Dr. King and I worked with Dr. Sam Anderson, Sandra Rivers and Dr. Don Smith to plan the first national gathering of conscious Black folks committed to education for liberation. A letter was sent to a select group of about 100 Black educators and activists from around the country to join us in a two-day planning convening in Atlanta, Georgia, for an NBEA Summit in a centrally-located city. About 45 courageous souls answered the call and attended the convening. They became known as The Atlanta 45. This powerful group of dedicated activists included the brilliant Dr. Iva Carruthers, founding General Secretary of the Dewitt Proctor Conference. A few weeks after the Atlanta convening, we asked Iva to chair a committee to identify a hotel in Chicago where the NBEA Summit could be held.

Before The Atlanta 45 showed up, we had already identified the "action" groups that we wanted people to work on. They included the school-to-prison pipeline, youth, parent engagement and a Black education online course. Another one was my vision of 1,000 African-centered schools. My idea was to select 100 schools each year (over a period of ten years) that would become part of a national network. The schools in this network would receive special professional development, help with grant writing, mini-grants for enrichment activities and access to a website where they could post best practices and share other news about their schools.

From the meeting in Atlanta, Dr. Sharroky Hollie emerged as the one most committed to helping me further formulate what "1,000 Schools" would look like. Because we had worked closely in California through the institutes at Stanford and he was the founder of a charter school that served predominantly Black students, he was a natural fit. Sharroky needed some additional help so I turned to Dr. John Browne. One of the most intelligent people I know, Dr. Browne worked with Sharroky, Caletha Pindle and myself to create the outline for the two-day session that ended up being at the Westin Hotel in Chicago in October 2012. Caletha came highly-recommended by Dr. King and she did not disappoint. In the months leading up to the summit, she faithfully lent her deep expertise.

The Summit was a huge success in spite of some internecine battles with the NBEA founders and being left with a $50,000 hotel bill. I will not go into the gory details here. About 200 warriors came from all over the country and some parts of Canada to help us begin to craft a 25-year education for liberation plan. The response to the "1,000 Schools" action team was very positive. Elizabeth Whittaker, the bright and dedicated principal at the time of Nsoroma Institute in Detroit, was such a valuable contributor to our session that I asked her to join our nascent Leadership Team. She agreed and hit the ground running. Over the next few months, the Leadership Team met and started working on the various components of "1,000 Schools" that were central to the building of a new organization. During this time period, I turned to Dr. King and Dr. Hassimi Maiga, a Songhoy language expert and chief from the African country of Mali, for an official name for "1,000 Schools" and they suggested A Black Education Network (ABEN). Dr. Maiga said that in the Songhoy language, "aben" means the buck stops here or it is finished. I loved the name because it accurately conveyed my sentiments that education for liberation should rest with our people, not others. In other words, the buck stops with us!

During this post-summit time, I worked on pulling together a Board of Directors and Wisdom Circle. I had met the charismatic Bernard Kinsey, founder of The Kinsey Collection, when he presented at our NBEA Summit in October 2012. After months of cultivating a relationship with him and his lovely wife, Shirley, and debonair son, Khalil, I asked Bernard if he would serve as chairman of ABEN. He agreed. This was a huge win for ABEN. The Kinsey Collection is a remarkable assemblage of Black art and artifacts that Bernard and Shirley have amassed over more than forty years of marriage. Select pieces of The Kinsey Collection have been at the Smithsonian, major museums around the country, and is currently at Epcot Center in Disney World. Millions of people have seen the exhibit and marveled at its contents. My favorite pieces include one of Phyliss Wheatley's original books of poetry and a letter from Malcolm X to Alex Haley (producer of the smash hit series from 1977 entitled *Roots* and author of the book by the same title). There is even a curriculum that accompanies the pieces and the plan is to use it to teach Black history in ABEN's schools.

I then asked Paul Griffin, who had helped underwrite the launch of the CAAAE years earlier, to serve as Vice Chair. He agreed. The Kinseys were opening one of their phenomenal exhibits at the Gannt Museum in Charlotte, North Carolina. They asked me to join them as their guest and generously sent me an airline voucher good for a round trip. The CAAAE covered my hotel rooms and I booked four nights at the local Westin. On the night of the grand opening, Bernard spoke after a lecture by Harvard professor—Dr. Henry Louis Gates. During the question and answer period, I mentioned how Bernard had agreed to be chairman of the board of ABEN as an example of his humility and commitment to Black people. Afterwards, Jillian Hishaw came up to me and said she would love to hear more about ABEN and work with us. She was accompanied by her close friend, Star Spencer. Both beautiful, sharp attorneys under 40, I was struck by their sincerity after spending some time talking with them and asked if they would join ABEN's board. They agreed. The board was shaping up nicely, but I needed a treasurer. When I returned to CA, I asked the CAAAE's accountant if he would serve in that role. He agreed. The last person who I added to ABEN's board was a long-time friend of mine who attended the same church in East Palo Alto, California, when he was working on his PhD at Stanford. Dr. Worku Negash had an illustrious career in higher education and took an early retirement to open a school in his native country of Ethiopia. We had been out of touch with each other for a few years when he Goggled my name, found my email address through the CAAAE's website and reached out. We discovered that we were living a few short miles away from each other. Ours was a warm and exciting reunion as we each shared about our passions and plans. He asked for my help in several areas related to his schools and I happily complied and I asked him to join ABEN's board as our international connection and he did not hesitate. ABEN's board was complete and I was pleased.

Because I know that funders pay close attention to an organization's board and we had a great inaugural one, I decided that we also needed a Wisdom Circle of widely-recognized Black educators and activists to further bolster ABEN's credibility. At the convening of The Atlanta 45, I was introduced to a national treasure—Dr. Adelaide Sanford. A Vice Chancellor Emerita with the New York Board of Regents, Dr. Sanford had served as principal for many years of one of the highest-performing schools in New York. It happened to be all Black. I was so moved by her vision for Elder's House in Selma, Alabama, that I wrote a check from the CAAAE's account for $1,000 shortly after her talk. Almost one year later, I spent some time with her at the Pettis Bridge-crossing Jubilee in Selma, Alabama, and had the privilege of learning more about why she is so revered among progressive Black educators. She was the first one I asked to join ABEN's Wisdom Circle. Soon after that, I attended an AERA convention and asked Drs. Lisa Delpit, Carol Lee and Gloria Ladson-Billings. Because I had established a great relationship with them when they keynoted the CAAAE's summer institutes and they really believed in our mission, they all agreed to serve. I needed some men so I reached out to Drs. John Browne and Wade Nobles and they both accepted. When I was at a Kellogg conference in North Carolina, I attended a session about bringing fresh vegetables to urban communities. One of the outstanding presenters was Malik Yakini from Detroit, Michigan. After his session, I spent time talking with him about his work. When we decided to have our second summit without the NBEA to mitigate the Westin Hotel bill of $50,000, we planned to induct elders into the Wisdom Circle there and I recommended Malik. He attended and I was really impressed with his humility and commitment to African people. In fact, he was one of the founders of the Nsoroma Institute where Elizabeth Whittaker was principal for two years before its untimely closing. Soon after the summit, I asked Elizabeth to ask him if he would be willing to serve as part of our Wisdom Circle and he agreed. We were strong. We were complete.

The other work I concentrated on, while Dr. Hollie and Dr. Browne were creating ABEN's application for membership, was fundraising. In order to fully implement ABEN, I had created a budget that required $1 million each year for 10 years. Having worked closely with the highly-effective Preschool California (now Early Edge Learning) which was established with a grant of $1 million per year for 10 years by the Packard Foundation, I knew that having a paid staff and guaranteed annual income from the onset would help an organization gain traction right away and sustain its efficacy. After our awesome graphic designer (Benita Lovett-Rivera), introduced to us at the gathering in Atlanta in 2012, put together a beautiful brochure describing ABEN's genesis, mission and vision statements, Ten Core Values, incentives for joining, board and wisdom circle members, it was time for me to "shop around" the idea. I got that opportunity when I responded to a blog that the relatively new president of the Hewlett Foundation, Larry Kramer, posted about wanting his constituents to give him candid feedback about their grant-making. I told him that Hewlett had one of the worse track records when it came to awarding grants to organizations run by people of color. They were great at serving children of color as long as White people handled the funds. I call this the slave-master syndrome. The "master" is not confident that the "slave" knows what is best for his own kind. I recommended that Mr. Kramer read the Greenlining

Institute's study where that dismal record was documented. I also said that I would be happy to meet with him to discuss what I called "The Color of Philanthropy" (see chapter 8). He replied the next day and said he would be happy to meet with me. I told him that in addition to discussing racism in philanthropy, I also wanted him to give me some candid feedback about ABEN's brochure. Having access to a foundation president of Mr. Kramer's stature is rare for people of color. I was so excited! Three weeks later, I sat in his office and had a wonderful and very candid conversation with a brilliant legal scholar who had served for eight years as dean of Stanford's law school before taking over the presidency at Hewlett. Although I was not there to make a formal "ask" for funding, Mr. Kramer offered to "seed" our work with at least $50,000 per year for three years or $100,000 per year for three years depending on his 2014 special projects budget. I was overjoyed not only due to his generosity, but also because it affirmed that my vision for ABEN was viable and worth funding. Mr. Kramer told me to call his office in mid-January and he would be able to tell me what size the grant would be. I followed up and he said that his budget was smaller than he anticipated, but that he could give the CAAAE $50,000 per year for three years to seed ABEN's work. In the weeks that ensued, his very professional staff expedited the process and decided to give us the total $150,000 at once so that we could just write one report after the three years and have access to all of the funds up front. This catapulted ABEN's work to another level of excellence. Not only was I able to pay some of the hard-working Leadership Team members and consultants who had donated countless hours to the development of ABEN, I was also able to host a retreat at the beautiful Asilomar Conference Center near the Pacific Ocean in Monterey, California. In addition to all members of the Leadership Team, we also have representatives from ABEN's board, its advisory committee and parent praxis team.

As though the $150,000 gift was not grand enough, I also took the time during my meeting with Larry Kramer to ask him if he knew the new Black president of the Ford Foundation—Darren Walker. I said that I wanted to ask Mr. Walker for the $10 million over a ten-year period to fund ABEN. We found favor again. Larry said that he had known Darren when they were practicing attorneys and had lunch with him a few months ago! I asked him if it would be OK for me to mention what financial support Hewlett had promised in my request for a meeting with Mr. Walker at his offices in Manhattan when I was going to be in Brooklyn a few months hence. Larry said to openly copy him on my email and he would gladly share with Darren about why he was financially supporting ABEN's work. I wrote the email. Mr. Walker sent a warm response two days later and in three months I was sitting in his beautiful office at the Ford Foundation. I liked Darren instantly. His office had beautiful African masks and among the many books piled on his conference table was Michelle Alexander's *The New Jim Crow*. I felt right at home. We warmly embraced and after 10 minutes we were high-fiving each other. After clarifying some questions he had about the ask, he said that he would need to send the "ask" to his executive team that considered "big ideas" on a regular basis. Fast forward. Although Ford did not fund ABEN, the door was left open for us to discuss the possibility of support through some other creative means once Ford finished its new strategic planning process. In the meantime, Mr. Walker authorized a grant to the CAAAE for $100,000 because he said he really was impressed with our work in California. I was so encouraged by yet another gift that just landed in our lap. This is all very rare in the philanthropic sector, but it does point to the importance of building great relationships with key decision-makers.

Earlier in this chapter, I mentioned that there was a second summit at the Westin in Chicago to mitigate the $50,000 hotel bill. Dr. Carruthers, Dr. King and myself planned this one. We actually called it A Black Education Congress. It attracted about 150 people from around the country and was just as powerful as the first summit. After the Congress and armed with the $150,000 for ABEN, we decided to hold strategy forums in each of the major regions of this country in 2014 so that more local warriors who could not afford a trek to Chicago could join our ranks. ABEN donated $5,000 for each regional so that we could also keep the cost to attend to a mere $25 per person. The southern regional one was held in Atlanta, Georgia, in April under the leadership of Dr. King and some of her doctoral students. She planned for about 40 people and close to 60 attended and enthusiastically participated in the praxis teams focused on some of the same topics from the NBEA Summit and A Black Education Congress. Held at the African-centered Sankofa Freedom Charter Academy in Philadelphia in September for the eastern region, just over 100 people attended including about 40 who came by bus from New York. What I called the "dream team" of planners produced a powerful forum: Dr. Kelli Mickens, Benita Lovett-Rivera, Khem Irby and Dr. Fatima Muid. I had the privilege of visiting Sankofa the day before the forum and was almost moved to tears by what I saw on their two campuses of elementary-aged children on one, and middle and high school students on another—joyful learners, well-behaved and proud of their African ancestry (just like at Sharroky's school—CLAS). It is the way all Black students should be taught. I helped coordinate the western regional forum with the remarkable president of the United Black Student Unions of California (Amauri Ross), co-founder of the inspiring African American Museum of Beginnings (Khalif Rasshan), and a faithful member of ABEN's Parent Praxis Team (Dr. A. Carl Duncan). With Bernard Kinsey kicking off the forum with a powerful presentation entitled "What You Did Not Learn in History Class," the audience of about 85 people were riveted and the tone was set for the day. After the day ended, a teacher from the Pomona Unified School District came up to me and said that the day helped her realize why she was so discouraged about her work. She had been parched and in need of what our forum offered. She said her soul had been watered. The next day I got a call from Onaje Muid who had attended the praxis session that I did for ABEN in Philadelphia. He was following up because he wanted me to know that he was still quite energized by the gathering and ready to work. I told him what the woman had said and he exclaimed, "We are the Water Carriers!" I added a tag line (bringing hope and inspiration to a parched people) and announced that I was naming ABEN's newsletter and blog "The Water Carrier". This is what community creates when our pathways are aligned. The fourth and final forum was held in Detroit at Paul Robeson, Malcolm X Academy in November for the mid-western region and spearheaded by the school's principal, Dr. Jeffrey Robinson, and the brilliant Dr. Geneva Smitherman.

The work of ABEN will positively affect millions of children long after I am in that ethereal place of slumber. **To be chosen as a vessel to uplift my people and equipped with an enormous capacity to do this work brings me great joy and fulfillment. Onward!**

Chapter 9

Lessons Learned on the Journey

When I told the Project WORD students that I was going to write a book about our four-year journey together, that is precisely what I planned to do. I was going to devote one chapter to each student and talk about how he or she traveled from ninth grade to twelfth. I realized that I would end up revealing too much personal drama if I went that route and I never wanted any students or their families to feel violated. To keep my word to the students, I decided to incorporate them into a larger frame around my journey as a Black teacher. That is how this memoir was born. When I was writing what was going to be the last chapter about A Black Education Network (ABEN), I realized that there were lessons I learned along the journey that were worth sharing as the final chapter of the book. Most people like neat lists and I am no exception. Once I decided to come up with a list of 10, they just tumbled out of my head.

Lesson 1: Thank people. As I look back on the three institutions that I started on a shoestring budget or no budget, I realize that getting people to work for me was easiest when I thanked them. It did not matter if it was the janitor at Yerba Buena High School in San Jose who opened the gym and classrooms for us so that we could host our STEM sessions for the Carver Scholars Program or the former superintendent of the Milpitas Unified School District, Paul Perotti, who agreed to serve as one of the presenters for the SCCABE's early Cultural Pursuits Awards Ceremony. Everyone matters. Bobbie Brooks frequently shares with me how I bend over backwards to "pamper" the CAAAE's board members with nice hotel stays, great food, and small gifts. She knows that it is my way of thanking them for the countless hours they volunteer to ensure that the CAAAE's mission is met. Sincerely thank people for even the smallest deed and watch how much more they will do for you.

Lesson 2: Affirm people. This actually goes hand in hand with thanking people. When you affirm a person's worth, it not only bolsters her self-esteem, it also helps build efficacy. This is most evident in the remarkable parents who have been and are currently in the STEM programs that I have coordinated. All parents have to commit to volunteering in the program throughout the length of their enrollment. Some parents, like David and Kelly

Johnson, enrolled their daughter (Shelby) when she was in kindergarten and Shelby graduated from high school in 2015. Early on, I recognized first Kelly's talent and then David's and they have been a remarkable duo. Kelly has served as president of our Operations Advisory Committee (OAC), which helps the STEM director run the GSP, for seven consecutive years. David is a professional musician and provides great entertainment at our annual science fairs. I could go on and on about other GSP parents who serve faithfully. Not only did I recognize parent/leaders each year at our science fair gala, I also made it a point of affirming their value to the GSP at every opportunity throughout the year. Affirming people is another way of letting them know that you could not do the work without them.

Lesson 3: Listen to people. In the early days of the CAAAE, the board consisted of a president, vice president, secretary, treasurer, and ten co-coordinators (two for each of our five regions at the time). One summer, all of the board members as well as some Advisory Board members (like Dr. Noma LeMoine) attended a retreat at Cypress to do a SWOT (Strengths, Weaknesses, Opportunities, Threats) analysis on the CAAAE. At the end of the two-day gathering when we were debriefing the process, one board member said that she was impressed that I would allow them to "take apart" the CAAAE after all of the hard work that I invest in it day in and day out. I told her that the organization did not belong to me and their SWOT was a great exercise for me to listen to constructive criticism and ways to improve going forward. Another example of the value of listening to people is when they candidly share with you character flaws that contribute to failed relationships. Growing up and into adulthood, I always wanted to get along with everyone. I was voted Class Personality during my senior year of high school because of my "likeable" nature. I never ate in the teacher's lounge so I did not have allegiances to any of the many cliques that were prevalent on the campuses where I taught. Yet there was also a side of me that could be caustic and harsh. I am ashamed to admit that I have reduced a few people to tears with some unkind, cutting words. As a result of listening to people like my daughter, Bobbie Brooks, Joyce King and Chris Norwood, I have become less rough around the edges. I have become less critical of people and their shortcomings and more compassionate.

Lesson 4: Believe in people. This is tied to the first three lessons. Many people write off Black parents as not interested in the education of their children. I never felt this way about any parents. From the onset of my teaching career, I leaned on my parents to help me steer their wayward children and to join me in praising them when they did well. Because of that mindset, it was natural to build the CSP with parental involvement at its foundation. I have not been disappointed. I let them know what my expectations are for them, give them some training and/or guidance and watch them soar. When you believe in people, they perform in ways that might even surprise you.

Lesson 5: Build alliances. This is probably one of the most critical pieces to the success of my institution-building. From my carefully cultivated relationship with Dr. T.J. Rodgers and Cypress for our STEM programs to my alliance with Dr. Linda Darling-Hammond and the Stanford University School of Education for our summer institutes to the knowledge I have gained through my affiliation with Bay Area Blacks in Philanthropy (BABIP), collaborating with like-minded people and organizations will lead to success. In addition to ABEN's board members and Wisdom Circle, some of my most valued allies are: Brad Strong of Children Now; Dr. Nancy Markowitz of the Center for Teaching and Reaching the Whole Child; Frances Wilson (my sister!) of the National Society of Black Engineers (NSBE); Benita Lovett-Rivera of The Mother's Agenda of New York (The MANY); David Sapp of Public Advocates; and Manny Barbara of the Silicon Valley Education Foundation. While some people would not characterize their funders as allies and there are many that I would not place in that category either, there are two who have gone beyond being "just" funders and are actually great thought partners—Larry Kramer, president of the Hewlett Foundation, and Castle Redmond, program officer of The California Endowment.

Lesson 6: Show results. Once each year, I make it a point of having a face-to-face meeting with Dr. T.J. Rodgers to give him updates on how his "investment" is faring. In addition to having full use of the building that houses Cypress' headquarters, the CAAAE also gets $10,000 annually from the company to help underwrite our science fair and gala. Early in our collaboration, I asked T.J. if he wanted a written report about how we were spending his donation. He said, "If I needed a written report, I would not give you the money. I see your results and that is all I need." In addition to the results of Project WORD, the GSP's are so impressive that the CAAAE has won a number of awards. The Lux Award from the Level Playing Field Institute and the STEM Innovation Award from the Silicon Valley Education Foundation are among the most recent. My leadership has been recognized by countless organizations ranging from the American Chemical Society to the Alpha Kappa Alpha Sorority. In 2014, I was awarded the Inez Jackson Legacy Award by the Silicon Valley NAACP in recognition of the enduring institutions that continue to make a positive impact on many families and their children. When you can show what your work has produced, people will notice and acknowledge you accordingly.

Lesson 7: Think big. From the time I became president of the SCCABE in 1994, I wanted to grow the organization in ways that it had never experienced. From increasing the outreach to districts to get more students honored for our annual Cultural Pursuits Awards Ceremony to partnering with the Healing Institute to launch the CSP, I was always thinking big. When I was selected to serve on the Implementation Oversight Team of a $34 million multi-agency School Linked Services initiative, I realized that the Black students in Silicon Valley would probably not benefit from the help because so few are enrolled in schools in that area. I envisioned having a "hub" that would deploy people to wherever Black children were in the Valley. I named the hub Imani Village. Imani is Swahili for faith and it means that we have faith in our children's abilities. Dr. Nancy Pena, chairperson of the School Linked Services initiative at that time, liked the idea and was prepared to allocate $250,000 per year for three years so that Imani Village could serve as a demonstration project for Black students in the Valley. An opportunity arose for more funds and expanded services for Imani Village through a partnership with Unity Care—a well-run nonprofit whose expertise is in providing housing and mental health services to foster care youth. Dr. Pena's idea was pitched to the Santa Clara County Board of Supervisors and it was unanimously approved with a $5.2 million contract over a 30-month period that began in March 2014. When you think beyond what is and push for what could be, great things can happen.

Lesson 8: Follow your passion. When I am asked to describe the work of the CAAAE, I usually say that it is unapologetically focused on serving Black students. I have always cared about all students who entered my classroom or were members of clubs that I advised, but my passion has been unwaveringly for children who look like me. For the first seven years of the CAAAE's and the GSP's existence, I never got paid even though I was putting in 40-hour weeks to coordinate both. When I asked Gloria Whitaker-Daniels to become the director of the GSP on a tiny stipend that she suggested, she had just left her job at Apple and enthusiastically threw herself into running it. Even after she took a full-time position at Amazon, she continued to give 1,000% to the GSP. It is her passion. Because I am so passionate about this work, I retired seven years early to focus on running the CAAAE full-time. Almost four years ago, Wanda Kurtcu attended the CAAAE's 2011 institute at Stanford. Ironically, Wanda and I had graduated from the same high school in the same year and had connected on Facebook a few months earlier. She was the educational technologist at the Dr. George Washington Carver Elementary School in San Francisco's low-income Bayview/Hunter's Point neighborhood. When I mentioned the GSP in my introductory remarks at the institute, Wanda's interest was piqued. At a break, she asked if the CAAAE could bring a program like that to Carver. Thanks to the support of Carver's principal, Natasha Flint-Moore, we were able to implement a school-based model there. Due to various reasons, in the 2014-2015 school year we decided to use the GSP's original Saturday model with the CSP. Due to my passion, I am now coordinating that site and loving it.

Lesson 9: Strive for excellence. With this wrong-headed focus on testing, children are labeled anywhere from far below basic to advanced. While many educators are pleased when children are at grade level, I have always insisted on a higher standard. Instead of settling for mediocrity, why not strive for excellence? When we were working on the CAAAE's vision statement, it was important to me to use the phrase "excellence for all" as a goal. If you shoot for the stars and land on the moon, you still have reached a lofty height. Study after study has shown that students often do not perform well academically in classes where the teacher has low expectations for them. No surprises here. Many people are content to check off that they accomplished a task or coordinated an event. Few evaluate the caliber of the task or the event. People will notice when you pursue excellence in all of your work even if you miss the mark from time to time.

Lesson 10: Work hard and smart. One reason for writing this book is to reflect on what God has equipped me to do and share my how-to journey. People often comment on my enormous capacity for work. I do work hard, but I have also learned to work smart. This means finding allies who can help advance your work and leveraging them. It means being courageous enough to seize opportunities like the one that lead to my meeting T.J. Rodgers at the Marriott Hotel or responding to Larry Kramer's blog. What do you have to lose? Yet you have so much to gain!

ABOUT THE AUTHOR

Debra Watkins, Founder, President and Executive Director, of California Alliance of African American Educators (CAAAE) E-mail: info@caaae.org.

Debra Watkins was born in Los Angeles and raised in Pomona, California. After her high school graduation, she studied in France for one year and earned a baccalaureate that enabled her to attend college in the country free of charge. Instead, she returned to the United States and earned a B.A. in English with minors in French and Psychology from Pitzer College in 1976. She then entered Stanford University's Teacher Education Program and earned a Master's degree in Education as well as Life-time Teaching Credentials in English, French and Psychology in 1977. A second Master's degree in Counselor Education was granted in 1996 from San Jose State University.

Debra had spent her entire career of 35 years in the East Side Union High School District (ESUHSD) of San Jose before retiring in May 2012. Debra taught high school English for 14 years, then helped start an alternative high school called Pegasus. After eight years at

Pegasus, she coordinated Project WORD (Working On Re-defining our Destiny) - a culturally responsive intervention program for African American students. While on an unpaid leave of absence from the ESUHSD, Debra worked one year as Director of Silicon Valley Service for a school reform organization called Partners in School Innovation. She was responsible for coaching elementary school principals and teachers on how to close the opportunity gap for Black and Brown students.

After being away from the classroom for five years, Debra returned for three years and taught juniors and seniors. As of July 2007, she is the full-time Executive Director of the California Alliance of African American Educators (CAAAE), an organization she founded in 2001. Debra was also one of the founding members of the Santa Clara County Alliance of Black Educators (SCCABE) approximately 30 years ago and served as its president for seven years (1994-2001). In 2007, the CAAAE partnered with the ESUHSD and garnered a four-year, $400,000 grant from the AT&T Foundation's Aspire program to fully implement Project WORD at Oak Grove High School. This grant was to ensure the on-time graduation of a cohort of African American freshmen. Project WORD was highly-successful and is a model for districts seeking to close the opportunity gap and reduce high school drop-out rates.

When Debra established the CAAAE in 2001, she also created the Dr. Frank S. Greene Scholars Program

(GSP). Named after an African American scientist who helped pave the way for today's computers, the GSP is a long-term, youth development STEM initiative for students of African ancestry based in Santa Clara County. With 100% of its students enrolling in college, 90% graduating in four years with a BS or BA degree, and 60% of those degrees in STEM fields (eight times the national average for Black students), the GSP has garnered the support of companies in Silicon Valley ranging from Google to Texas Instruments to Cisco and Intel. Headquartered at Cypress Semiconductor, the GSP hosts the only all-African American science fair in the state of CA. In 2011, the CAAAE created a school-based model at the Dr. George Washington Carver Elementary School in the Bayview/Hunter's Point neighborhood of San Francisco.

In the 2015-2016 school year, Debra partnered with two internationally-renowned Black educators and funded their work that is now touching hundreds of additional students in San Jose. With Tony Browder, she helps coordinate the Cultural Imperative Initiative at Mt. Pleasant, Independence and Santa Teresa high schools.

The next generation of Debra's work is national. She is the founder of A Black Education Network (ABEN). Her vision is to support/develop/sustain a network of 1,000 schools and school communities in the United States, selected over a ten year period, that are committed to academic and cultural excellence for Black students.

Debra has garnered countless awards for her work, serves on local, regional and statewide committees and boards, and has helped raise several millions of dollars for the CAAAE since its inception. Some of those funds were used to help convene two national gatherings of progressive Black educators—both at the Westin Airport Hotel in Chicago in 2012 and 2013. The CAAAE is considered the "go-to" organization for issues involving Black students in the state of CA.

CAAAE

www.caaae.org

ABEN

www.aben4ace.org

GSP

www.greenescholars.org

My Senior Year at Ganesha High School

Mama Sallie

My Mother's Mother

Mrs. Schneider was my 11th grade Black literature teacher. She was wonderful and opened our eyes to so much!

I was a cheerleader at Ganesha High School!

This is my junior year of high school. I was always in the yearbook next to Rocky Mayer!

143

Z CLUB

The Z Club was a service club for smart girls!

FUTURE TEACHERS OF AMERICA

One year, I was Vice President of the Future Teachers of America Club at my high school.

Mrs. Alberts
9th Grade
Algebra Teacher

Mr.Kelly, 9th Grade
English Teacher

Mr. Wooten, International Relations Teacher

Mrs. Brink, 12th Grade English Teacher

Mama, Brotha and Frances

Mama as High School Graduate

My Dad's mother, Irene Matthews – her first name is my middle name

Papa and Mother with Daddy and his Sisters

148

Daddy with Me on My Wedding Day

Mama and Me at an awards ceremony
She was very proud of the accomplishments of all
of her children.

Debra and Alicia

*Son-in-law Patrick, Granddaughter Imade,
Daughter Alicia a few years ago*

For information about special discounts for bulk purchases, please contact CAAAE at (408)977-4188 or info@caaae.org.

Debra Watkins is available for live events and speaking engagements. For more information, or to book your event, contact (ABEN), P.O. Box 3134, San Jose, CA 95156, or at (408)977-4188, or email at: info@caaae.org.

CAAAE

www.caaae.org

ABEN

www.aben4ace.org

GSP

www.greenescholars.org